Philip Hesketh is a psychology graduate who enjoyed a highly successful sales career at Procter & Gamble. In 1986 he was creator, Managing Partner and New Business Director of Advertising Principles, an advertising agency that has grown into a multi-million pound business. Having spent his entire working life studying and practicing persuasion and influence, Philip is now a speaker on 'The Psychology of Persuasion'.

He mixes thought-provoking, well-researched, persuasive techniques with his own highly entertaining, unique brand of humour. The result? Audiences leave Philip's events inspired and better informed on how buying, selling, persuading and influencing actually work.

For more information, visit the author's web site at www.heskethtalking.com

life'sagamesofixtheodds guarantees that you will be more liked by more people – and more persuasive as a result. It is anecdotal, solidly researched and will have you laughing out loud. You will win more friends, be more influential, make more money and get your own way more often after reading this book. You will learn:

- The seven psychological reasons behind why and how we are persuaded and how to use them to your advantage

- The importance of seeing the relationship from the other person's point of view

- How to develop worthwhile, profitable relationships

- The keys to building trust and credibility

- How to be more liked by more people and get your own way more often

- How to develop the skills to overcome obstacles and reduce conflict

- The psychology of the NAIL persuasion and influence process.

CAPSTONE
be inspired!

Life's a Game So Fix the Odds

Life's a Game So Fix the Odds

How to Be More Persuasive and Influential in Your Personal and Business Life

Philip Hesketh

CAPSTONE

Published in 2005 by Capstone Publishing Limited (a Wiley Company), The Atrium, Southern Gate, Chichester, West Sussex, PO19 8SQ, UK
Phone (+44) 1243 779777

Email (for orders and customer service enquires): cs-books@wiley.co.uk
Visit our Home Page on www.wiley.co.uk or www.wiley.com

Other Wiley Editorial Offices

John Wiley & Sons, Inc. 111 River Street, Hoboken, NJ 07030, USA
Jossey-Bass, 989 Market Street, San Francisco, CA 94103-1741, USA
Wiley-VCH Verlag GmbH, Pappellaee 3, D-69469 Weinheim, Germany
John Wiley & Sons Australia Ltd, 42 McDougall Street, Milton, Queensland 4064, Australia
John Wiley & Sons (Asia) Pte Ltd, 2 Clementi Loop #02-01, Jin Xing Distripark, Singapore 129809
John Wiley & Sons Canada Ltd, 22 Worcester Road, Etobicoke, Ontario, Canada, M9W 1L1

Wiley also publishes its books in a variety of electronic formats. Some content that appears in print may not be available in electronic books.

Library of Congress Cataloging-in-Publication Data is available

British Library Cataloguing in Publication Data

A catalogue record for this book is available from the British Library

ISBN-13: 978-1-84112-682-1 (PB)
ISBN-10: 1-84112-682-9 (PB)

Typeset in Palatino 11/15pt by Sparks Computer Solutions, Oxford (www.sparks.co.uk)
10 9 8 7 6 5 4

FSC
Mixed Sources
Product group from well-managed forests and other controlled sources
Cert no. SGS-COC-2953
www.fsc.org
© 1996 Forest Stewardship Council

Contents

Preface

It's often said that nothing under the sun is really new; there are just new twists on existing themes. So when I set out to write a book on persuasion – a subject that's been around ever since early caveman first encouraged his fellow cave dwellers to see things his way with the aid of a big club – I admit to being a little apprehensive. At one point I even considered the idea of setting up a 'Plagiarism Advice Bureau' to counter any criticism. But then I guess somebody has already done that too. The bottom line is that you just don't know if someone has had the same idea as you.

Throughout this book I make three Biblical references, and the first one is coming up right now. It's from Ecclesiastes: 'There is no new thing under the sun. Who is he that shall speak and say, "Behold, this is new"? It has already been in the ages that have passed before us.'

What Ecclesiastes would make of microwaves, mobile phones and laptops I don't know. What I do know is that *he* thought there was nothing new under the sun all those years ago. And what *I* know is that the information, thoughts and ideas in *Life's a Game So Fix the Odds* fall into three categories.

Firstly, like everyone else, I learn from other people. I have read books, attended seminars and worked with colleagues all my life. Some people have given me a single thought that has stuck with me for life; some have written books that I have read and been impressed by. Others I have listened to, and found their words thought-provoking to the extent that they changed my life. Sometimes they meant to change my life; sometimes they didn't.

Secondly, there's the stuff in the book that is undoubtedly mine. I was in *that* shop, I attended *that* meeting and I had *that* experience. I observed what was happening to me; I looked on at other people's reaction and drew my own conclusions.

And thirdly, there is the stuff that I write about and I genuinely don't know if it's mine or if I got it from someone else. If you, dear reader, think that I got something from you, please e-mail me and I will give you due credit. In the meantime, in alphabetical order, here are the people that I would genuinely like to thank for their contribution to my thought processes. Of these six people, I have only met two personally.

Dale Carnegie's book *How to Win Friends and Influence People* was my starting point 35 years ago. That one book has been the biggest single influence on my life. Thank you, Mr Carnegie.

When I was researching and working on why people buy things and why people do what they do, I stumbled across Robert Cialdini's book *Influence* and found that he had already done an appreciable amount of work on what I was endeavouring to do. Accordingly, I have unashamedly taken on board many of his findings, thoughts and excellent work, and I wish to give him full credit for his contribution to my psychological reasons. I urge you to read *Influence*.

Steven Covey's classic *The Seven Habits of Highly Effective People* has also been an inspiration to me and I regard his work as one of the top ten business books of all time.

I have seen Robin Fielder of Leadership Development Ltd present on a number of occasions and his style, personality, content and integrity have impressed me every time. It is probably over 20 years since I saw him present 'Close That Sale!'. He has been presenting excellent seminars for many years and he has influenced me enormously.

My very good friend Steve McDermott, author of *How to be a Complete and Utter Failure in Life, Business and Everything* has been my inspiration and mentor for over ten years and a 'thank you' in a preface could not possibly do him justice. He is an excellent speaker, a great writer but, more importantly, an all-round decent bloke.

I also wish to give credit to Professor Gerald Zaltman of Harvard University. He inspired me to think differently about the brain and

I would strongly recommend you read one of his many books, *How Consumers Think*.

Finally, no preface is complete without a 'thank you' to the people who matter most to the author. This book, as with everything I do, every breath I take and, of course, every pound I make, is dedicated to my darling wife and my three wonderful sons.

PART I

The Starting Point – People, Beliefs and Relationships

CHAPTER I

Daring to Begin

It is Wednesday, February 25, 2004, and I am sitting overlooking the bay in Russell, Bay of Islands, New Zealand. It's a lovely summer's day with just a little cloud. An early morning walker ambles by; the ducks float happily and the world is at one.

For me it is an epiphanic moment.

My story is of a lifetime of the study of persuasion, influence, communication and relationships. I have been fascinated by how and why we do what we do. Though one is never sure, I think that the process of study began when a neighbour of my parents in Ashton-under-Lyne gave me a copy of Dale Carnegie's *How to Win Friends and Influence People*. It was at that stage and age – I guess 16 or so – that I decided to live my life with the principles of the book in mind. Some 34 years later, in my first year as a professional speaker on the subject of the psychology of persuasion, I vowed not to write a book until I could write one that was better than the book I had read all those years before. Carnegie's book rightly remains a classic. You are the better for reading it.

But I had also set myself a number of goals in deciding to become a professional speaker. One was to play live with Ralph McTell – more of him later. Another was to become the best and most sought-after speaker on the planet, bar none; the third was to be a professor at Harvard and speak at the likes of Oxford, Cambridge and Yale Universities. The fourth was to write a best-selling book and the fifth was to change the weather in February. If you know the north of England you will understand why.

And so I sit in the Bay of Islands in the North Island of New Zealand having achieved, for the time being, one of my goals.

I have changed the weather for *me*.

And that's what this book is about. It is to help you become more persuasive and influential. It is to help you get your own way more often. It is about understanding how the process of influence works and thereby making yourself happier by achieving *your* goals. It is also about challenging yourself to decide what those goals are. It is about you deciding your own equivalent of changing the weather in February and how to achieve it.

For you.

Life is a game and this book helps you to improve the odds.

But I said that I would not write a book until I could write a better one than Dale Carnegie's classic. So why now? Will it be better? I don't know. But I do know four things.

Firstly, there may never be a better time than this one. There's a lovely song by Paul McCartney called 'This One'. In it, he sings:

> Did I ever take you in my arms,
> Look you in the eye, tell you that I do?
> Did I ever open up my heart and let you look inside?
> If I never did it, I was only waiting, for a better moment that
>   didn't come.
> There never could be a better moment than this one, this one.

So, as the Romans used to say, *carpe diem* – or 'seize the day'.

So I'm taking my own advice. I'm daring to begin.

Secondly, I have been asked too many times by people where they can buy my book. Surely, they say, you must have written a book about all this? Where's the CD? Is there something I can take away to help me remember what I have learned today?

Thirdly, life and happiness are about the journey and not the destination. In my previous life as an ad man for 25 years I was often asked the question, 'How do I become a director?' My answer was always, 'Start behaving like one now.' So I begin this book because I can. Because I can't think of a better time to start this book than when it is dark and snowing in England in February and I am overlooking the bay in Russell having just finished breakfast.

And finally, an apology.

In all the time I have been speaking on the subject of influence and persuasion I have been of the view that there is no need to use swear words. The English language is rich and deep and there are, I do appreciate, many words you can use when you feel that something is nonsense. Whether it's an idea, a belief, or a point of view. You disagree, you think it's wrong?

A lot wrong.

In fact, you think it's rubbish. You get my drift? But despite my best efforts, I can't find a word that effectively conveys what my dad would call 'absolute balderdash'. So I invented a word.

'Horrocks'. It means that I think that a theory or view is horribly wrong. I'm afraid, dear reader, I use it 16 times in this book including this one here.

Bear with me.

So let's start at the beginning and discuss what persuasion and influence are all about.

CHAPTER 2

The Role of the Subconscious in Buying, Selling and Believing

Along with five partners, I set up an advertising agency in 1986 called Advertising Principles. In the ensuing years we handled some major brands. I was the new business guy. And the thing that always fascinated me more than anything was how brands worked. That is to say, how consumers have beliefs about brands. And indeed, in some cases, blind faith in a brand. We used to do the '625 Test' – more of that later – for a beer brand, which probably best illustrated how people believe in brands (i.e. an idea) and continued to believe in it, despite being faced with subsequent, overwhelming evidence that contradicted their belief. It's a bit like believing in Father Christmas when you are little.

I loved Father Christmas.

I truly believed he existed and loved me. I'd seen him. My parents, friends, aunts and uncles all told me he was real and I trusted them to tell the truth. And what better evidence was there than on the morning of December 25? 'He's been!' Thing is – I don't want to ruin it for you here – but it wasn't true, was it? It was just a belief. Many people have beliefs that aren't true. People believe not only in their chosen brands but also in their chosen opinions. Or sometimes the opinion that was given to them by their mother, father, favourite uncle, or even old boss who promised, 'If I want your opinion, I'll give it to you.' They – and you – have all sorts of beliefs and if you're going to become more persuasive as a result of reading this book, we need to start here.

With beliefs.

Your beliefs. The beliefs of the people you want to persuade. Because it doesn't matter whether the beliefs are true or not. People have beliefs. And they are held in the subconscious.

In the summer of 2001, 15 years after setting up Advertising Principles, I enrolled on a course at Harvard Business School. That had been one of my goals since the mid-90s. After all, if I was to be a professor at Harvard, I needed to study there as a starting point. I also set myself the goals of playing live with Ralph McTell, being the best professional speaker on the planet, going to New Zealand and, of course, changing the weather in February. One of my partners at Advertising Principles, Bernie May, came with me. And the lecture I most remember was when Professor Gerald Zaltman was speaking on the subject of the subconscious.

'Ninety-five per cent of our thoughts are subconscious,' he said.

'WOW!' I thought. That means 95% of our thoughts are not in our control! Frankly, I doubted him. I thought he'd made it up. So I put my hand up and asked the question. 'How do we know it's 95%, Professor Zaltman? Why *that* figure?'

He paused. 'Do you mean beyond the fact that I, professor at Harvard, who have written 14 books on the subject, am a past President of the Association for Consumer Research, have an AB from Bates College, an MBA from the University of Chicago, a PhD from the John Hopkins University and am widely regarded as the world's leading authority on the subconscious, say so?'

Oh dear.

You know those times when you've put one foot in and there's no getting it out again? You have foolishly said something that if you'd thought about it a little more you would never, ever say? He basically changed the lecture and told us about the subconscious. The point being that what people *say* they do isn't necessarily what they *actually* do. I sat in, or listened to, dozens and dozens of focus groups when I worked in advertising and I drew three conclusions. Firstly, most people, most of the time, don't know why they do what they do. Secondly, they don't really know why they buy what they buy. And thirdly, that people lie! Not always consciously, either. People interpret events in different ways. How they see things is not how you see things.

For instance, people may say what they think the researcher wants them to say; or say what will impress others. People often struggle to understand themselves and why they've done what they have. Even 'accompanied shops' have enormous flaws. That's when a shopper is escorted by a researcher, who prompts them and asks them why they're choosing one brand over another. And, on top of all that, most people don't know why they are doing what they are doing anyway!

Take personal care and beauty products such as perfumes and cosmetics. They invoke deep thoughts and feelings about what Professor Zaltman calls 'social bonding'. You will know more about how an individual really feels about the product by how it is gripped in the hand than by what people say about it. The whole body language communication (more of that later) is far more believable than the words and the tone of voice. Professor Albert Mehrabian's 1960s studies, which concluded that '55% of communication is through body language, 38% is tone of voice and 7% is the actual words spoken, is horrocks.

I think so. For goodness' sake; The Beatles were top of the charts with 'Paperback Writer' when he published his work. It's a long time ago. However, this out-of-date principle has stood the test of time because we all understand that it's the body language in which we believe. That is to say, what we give away by how we act and react.

Often, my wife doesn't need to say anything to communicate. Words aren't even 1%. Yet when we are in rapt attention and learning something very new, very relevant and of high interest, body language and tone count for little. You see, when you are trying to persuade someone, particularly of something quite radical, they will always see and perceive it in terms of their own personal frame of reference. And if you don't understand – or at least begin to appreciate – their frame of reference you will struggle to get through.

When, in response to his own question at the Institute of Directors' dinner in 1991, Gerald Ratner said, 'People ask me how can we afford to make this stuff so cheap and I say because it's absolute crap,' he couldn't have known what kind of frame of reference he was setting up for us all. Now, hidden deep in our subconscious mind is a frame of reference that Ratner equals crap. It's probably in the same 'box' as Roy Keane equals prawn sandwiches and Brentfords equals nylons, and certain people's deep-seated beliefs from their Catholic childhood that God is a Catholic and therefore anyone who is not a Catholic will not be able to enter Heaven. Or at the very least, you won't get a good seat. But the fact is, we all have these beliefs and they're held in the subconscious and it doesn't matter whether or not they're true. If we believe them we look for evidence to support our beliefs and we usually find it.

So persuasion is not just about turning features into benefits (more of that horrocks later), but about understanding as much as we can about how the mind of our persuadee thinks.

I was in town recently in a menswear store. The owner of the shop asked me if I wanted any help. 'No thanks,' I said. 'I'm just browsing.' And as I was doing just that another guy came in with his 'significant other'. They were smartly dressed, and as they walked into the shop the owner again said, 'Can I help you?' The gentleman smiled and said, in a very polite way, 'I'm looking for a Boss suit. I like the brand Boss. Do you sell Boss?'

Now he didn't sell Boss. So what would you do if you were the guy who owns the shop? Let me give you three options:

1   Tell the customer that you don't sell Boss but you know where he could find it.
2   Say that you agree that Boss is a fine brand, that you can understand why he likes it and although you don't sell it yourself you have something similar.
3   Ask him what in particular he likes about the Boss brand so that you have the best chance of matching his need to something you do have in the shop.

Clearly option 1 is helpful but you have little or no chance of making a sale. And you are reading this book, I hope, because you want to sell more, make more money and hold your price better. Option 2 is a much better answer but you're still guessing; whilst option 3 is clearly the best option. But the lesson of this whole book, if you want to skip the rest of the chapters and find the 'key', the 'nugget', the 'kernel' is this: *listen people into a sale.*

Shall I tell you what the shop owner actually did? He shot back at him, 'We all like Boss sir, but can you afford their prices?' The guy looked him straight in the eye and said, 'Yes I can.' And promptly walked out of the shop!

You can't insult people and hope to persuade them. One can only guess as to how many people the customer told that story over the coming weeks. People who were potential customers for our friendly menswear store that relies on personal recommendation! Will he ever go back? Go back to a shop that questions his ability to be able to buy a particular brand?

The point is that the potential buyer had a belief. His belief was – and almost certainly *still is* – that Boss is an excellent brand and it's the brand for him. The belief is a deep-rooted one and it's also an emotional one. He likes people who also like Boss because people like people who a) are like them, b) like what they like and c) have similar beliefs. So the starting point for persuasion is to accept that the other person's belief system may be quite different to yours. And if you are going to persuade them to do what *you* want them to do, you need to find out more about *their* beliefs and views. You need to know what they believe in. You need to know what *motivates* them.

For now, I want you to imagine that you're riding a horse. The horse is 95% of the whole and you are the other 5%. The horse is the subconscious mind and you, the rider, are the conscious mind. Later in the book we will look at ways you can train your horse but, for now, whenever you are reading this book and thinking of how to apply the techniques I shall share with you, I want you to imagine that the person you wish to persuade is on a horse. If you are to persuade the person to change their opinion and buy into your idea, it's like asking them to change the direction and speed of the horse. And, get this, the person you are trying to persuade is not in control of his horse!

Makes it a bit tricky now, doesn't it?

But that is what persuasion is all about.

It's not just turning features into benefits and hoping the other person 'gets it'. It's not just presenting your case. It's about under-standing how your horse – your own subconscious – gives away what you are thinking to the other person. It's about seeing how the other person's horse reacts. It is also about understanding that you have to persuade the other person's horse.

It is the subconscious, or the 'cognitive unconscious', that explains why decisions are emotional.

People buy emotionally and justify logically. Indeed, all decisions are made emotionally. The justification can be terribly logical but the decision to buy is emotional. The justification process after having bought is what we learned in psychology as 'cognitive dissonance'. Logic is the language of and for the conscious mind. Emotion is the language of and for the subconscious mind.

The banking and credit industry would be structured very, very differently if we only bought logically. If no one needed 'retail therapy'. If we only bought what we could afford. If we only bought what we needed and not what we wanted.

I love the whole concept of placebos. Who's kidding whom here? You are *told* a particular prescription will be good for you – and your horse believes it – and, hey presto, so often the 'miracle drug' – which is just a sugar pill – actually improves your physical condition. You just trained your own horse by tricking it into believing that you will get better!

When I was a Boy Scout we used to go on camping holidays. The Scout Leader was Alan Fish. Alan hadn't done a degree in psychology but he knew a thing or two about small boys. He bought dozens of aspirins and put them in 10 different small boxes. He carefully labelled the boxes according to different parts of the body. There were 'knee pills', 'headache pills', 'back pills' and so on.

If a boy had an injury, cut or bruise Alan would painstakingly go through all the boxes to make sure he got the right pill. The 'specialist' pill for the ailment. And it appeased every one of us. There was a bit of a to-do when a lad fell on his coccyx but apart from that it worked quite well.

It was probably my introduction to psychology.

I'm fascinated by how the subconscious works. I'm fascinated by people who say things like: 'I've tried to give up smoking but I can't'. When you keep saying that, who's the person who hears you the most?

You!

And your horse holds the belief that you can't give up smoking. Ever.

I'm fascinated by how my own subconscious works. If I need to wake up early to catch a plane or a train, I always wake up early. I have trained my horse to do so without any effort!

I'm also fascinated by persuasion and influence and how it works ...

CHAPTER 3

How to be More Liked by More People

I used to work in a bakery on Saturdays when I was at school in Ashton, Lancashire. Not only did I get to earn a day's pay and still be finished in time to play football in the afternoon but I also got to drive a big van. It was so old you had to 'double-declutch', and I would drive around from market to market delivering bread, buns, cakes and what my mother endearingly referred to as 'fancies'. We started promptly at 6 a.m. and I would leave home to walk to the bakery at half-past five. It fascinated me that everyone at that hour said 'hello' to each other. At that early hour in the morning there were only a few souls about and there was always an acknowledgement. By seven o'clock or so, the effect ended simply because there were more people about.

Whenever I'm running now (my sons call it jogging but I like to refer to it as running) there is always a nod of the head from other runners. An acknowledgement. Because we're doing the same thing. When I took my sons to university the other dads and I would always acknowledge each other as we carried the hi-fi and books and other accoutrements of student life into the halls of residence. Not only were we doing the same thing but we tended to be dressed alike too. What I call the 'Tony Blair School of Casual Wear for the Over-40s': chinos, deck shoes and an open necked, button-down denim shirt.

What this illustrates is that people like people who are like them. People like people who dress and behave like they do. Smokers have a 'thing' because they're alike. In meetings it's 'nice' to have a coffee together. Not because you need the coffee but because you are sharing an experience.

You are 'alike'.

When golfers meet, the conversation naturally turns to handicaps. Now, I'm not what you would call a 'natural' at golf. I think it's God's way of making me humble. But when a golfer I've just met asks me my handicap I seem to get one of two reactions. If they're a good golfer – my definition is they have at least one hole where they're expected to get a par – they react with an 'oh dear' expression. They are not eager to play with me because I'm not like them. Conversely, if their handicap is in the 20s they tend to slap me on the back, shake my hand and say something like, 'That's great – we're both rubbish – we must have a game!'

The whole purpose of the handicap system is to allow golfers of different abilities to play against each other and enjoy the competition. So why is that?

Because people like people who are like them. People like people who dress and behave like they do. Now, you can only do so much about how you look but you can do a lot about how you dress. And, just as importantly, what you share with others about what you believe in. People like people who agree with them. People like people who mirror their actions and body language. People like people who respect their beliefs and values. Those might include the importance of time-keeping, having clean shoes or just not saying, 'I hate dogs' when it's manifestly obvious they are a dog lover.

It's the things we have in common with people that help create the relationship and the differences that make them interesting and/or irritating.

Have you ever been to a football match and been part of a Mexican Wave? A nice feeling of doing something together – we are alike. Then the men in suits and ladies in hats in the directors' box don't participate. Because they are saying they are not like us.

And we don't like people who don't want to be like us and do what we are doing. So we boo them!

Watch those same people in that crowd enter a church, a library, a hospital waiting room or an expensive hotel. We behave as we do not only because we think we should, but because everyone else is acting in a hushed, reverent manner.

People like people who truly listen to them. People like people who flatter them and talk about their interests. People like people who remember their name. People like people who show a real and genuine interest in them. People like people who are like them.

Birds of a feather flock together.

Regrettably there's a flipside to that coin. People often don't like people for no other good reason than they're *not* like them: take race relations, religions and bigotry down the ages. Wars have been caused, continue to be fought, and the root of it is often simply that people don't like people who are not like them. They don't believe in the same things. I live in Yorkshire and was born and raised in Lancashire. It's over 500 years since Henry VII married Princess Elizabeth of York, uniting the warring Houses, but the rivalry remains. Because people like to 'belong' and the natural corollary to belonging is disliking the people who *don't* belong. Footballer Alan Smith was worshipped at Elland Road. Then he moved from Leeds United to Manchester United and the same people who adored him now hate him. Sol Campbell, Tottenham to Arsenal; Mo Johnston, Celtic to Rangers. Same guys, different shirts. Let's get back to the positive side …

So should you be a chameleon? Because the key thing about this is that people are far easier to persuade if they like you. The essence of selling is to make it easier for people to buy and the process starts with the relationship. And that, in turn, starts with how much they like you and respect you.

So what are the key issues here? Well, let's get into first impressions.

There is no doubt we all form first impressions quickly. A whole host of research projects have been undertaken to discover exactly how long it takes to form a lasting first impression. My summary is that 90% of the time, 90% of people form 90% of their first impression of you within 90 seconds. And, typically, before you've spoken, what you wear, the way you've walked and held yourself are the key elements to that first impression. And if you're going to persuade someone you have never met before then you need to think about all those issues.

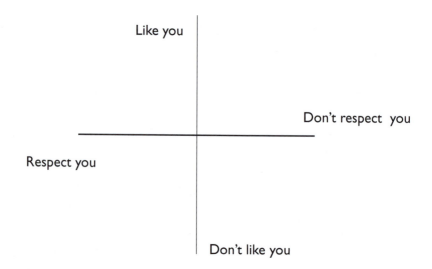

Figure 3.1 *First impressions*

I believe that people effectively 'plot' you on a scale that has 'Like you/Don't like you' on the vertical axis and what might best be described as 'Respect you/Don't respect you' on the horizontal axis (see Figure 3.1).

There is, of course, another axis. It's referred to sometimes as 'Love at first sight'. The French refer to it as 'The Thunderclap'. It's about love and lust and passion. It's the degree of instant physical and sexual attraction between two people. 'Chemistry'.

I'll go back to that later but for the purpose of this book I'm happier to leave that real love and waves lashing over the rocks thing to Mills & Boon.

Anyway, despite the fact that you can, of course, change your opinion of someone (and he or she of you), the initial opinion that is formed is immovable. Have you ever heard someone say, 'I never liked him from the beginning'?

Persuasion begins with the relationship. And that, in turn, begins with the first impression. When I worked in advertising, no company ever appointed our agency. People at the company appointed the people at the agency.

Because people buy people first. The press release would always say something like 'We very much liked the agency's strategic input and the creative solutions were radical, innovative and on brief blah blah blah.' We almost always, like every other agency and PR company, wrote the quote ourselves and although there was some truth in it, the real truth was that the people at the client end liked the people at the agency.

They *liked* them.

They could relate to them. They had confidence in them. And, yes, they thought they would deliver the creative product.

When I worked in Newcastle I represented an ad agency called Riley Advertising. I went to see a lady called Josie Pottinger at a large local company. We had three or four meetings and at that tender age and stage of my career I couldn't work out why she didn't want to use our agency. We were nearer geographically, could offer a better service at a reduced price and could offer a number of benefits over their London-based agency. But she didn't appoint us and when I left to work for the office in Manchester I introduced her to my replacement in Newcastle, Norma Barclay. Within a month Norma had won the account and the 1% commission that went with it. I was obviously a little frustrated and curious and asked Norma to chat to Josie and find out what the final straw had been. You know what Josie said? 'I always thought Phil made a lot of sense. I could see we would get a better service at a better price. I was sure it would be a sound decision. I just didn't particularly like him.'

Oh no!

Not that she didn't like me, but that I didn't *spot* she didn't like me! Because people buy people first. The first impression really counts in the persuasion process. And it's the non-verbal signals that matter in making the first impression.

I read recently that Prince Charles holds and plays with his cuff links in the way that he does because he's 'chained to the monarchy'.

Horrocks. It's just displacement activity. It's just something to do because he's a little nervous. But that 'something to do' gives you away. So, how do we tell if our body is sending the right signals? And how do we read others?

Basically, if you're bored, you're likely to be boring. If you don't really want to be somewhere your body gives it away. Enthusiasm is contagious and it's communicated by body language. If you don't have any enthusiasm, get another job.

If you want to know what someone thinks of you, look at his or her eye movement. When we first meet someone we tend to look from eye to eye; across the bridge of the nose. If you've ever wondered where to look when you are meeting someone in a business situation, simply look at the gap between his or her eyes at the bridge of the nose. You don't want to stare because it embarrasses them, but you don't want to be constantly averting your gaze because they begin to distrust you. (This is all going on in their subconscious, by the way!)

Interestingly, with friends, the gaze tends to drop below eye level and moves into a triangle shape around the two eyes and the mouth.

And if a couple start getting into what my mother calls 'a bit of something going on' the triangle gets bigger. It widens at the bottom and they start to look at each others' mouths. So if you want to know if someone likes you in *that* way, look to see if they're staring at your mouth. If they are, they subconsciously want to kiss you …

It's a well-researched fact that if someone likes you in an attractive sort of a way, their pupil size increases and so does their blink rate. So if you find someone attractive and want to test them out, increase your blink rate. If they feel the same way about you they'll unconsciously begin to match your blink rate. It's called 'mirroring' and, get this – they won't know they're doing it!

So people like people who are like them. And people are easier to persuade if they like you. So how do you 'cheat'? How do you get them to like you? Particularly if physically and perhaps age-wise, you're not that alike?

Mirroring.

Basically you do whatever they do. If they fold their arms and lean against a door, do that. If they lean forward in an 'I'll confide in you' sort of a way, then lean forward too. When they reach for their cup of coffee so do you. If they stroke their chin and look pensive follow them. If their feet point towards you, they are being open – so follow them.

But not too close, or else it looks like you've read a book or been on a course!

The secret is to let them feel that they're on the same 'wavelength' as you. To give them the impression we understand their mood and circumstance and truly empathize with it. Do it. It works. Now *you* know but *they* don't.

Unless they've read the book too.

And sometimes it's just natural, isn't it? Sometimes it feels as though we are numbers on the radio dial. You meet someone and you know you are on the same frequency. But this book and the benefit I hope you get from it apply when it's not so natural. Not everyone likes everyone else easily. For all of us some people are easier than others. The thing is if you want to be more persuasive you need people to like you more. Even when it's not so natural.

There's a flipside to 'love at first sight' too, isn't there?

When love is over and the embers are all that is left of the fire that once burned, and all the signals are clear, we often tend to avoid them. Sometimes lovers just drift apart and it's as natural as the tide going out just as the tide comes in. When you are lying beside the one you once loved is when you feel the most alone. And we avoid the feelings and the little voice that talks to us, just as we try to avoid an unpleasant time. We know it's coming but we don't want to face it. Complicated stuff, love. Let's get back to persuasion.

When we come to the section in the book on negotiation, one of the key things is to be fully aware of what your body is saying to the other person. An important lesson there: do not to let your body do what it naturally wants to do.

But just before we go into more detail of how you improve the impression people have of you, remember that *you* are always forming an opinion of the person you are meeting too; and let me give you this thought:

Last year, £17 billion was inherited by British individuals. We are the first generation to benefit in such enormous numbers from our parents having property, and it was the buying of property in the 1950s and 1960s that is now triggering the largest transfer of wealth in the history of money. First impressions have always been deceptive but even more so now if you're wondering if somebody's got enough money to buy your product or service. In other words, don't *you* judge the book by the cover.

So what are the key issues for making a good first impression?

- Be 'appropriate', on time and reduce the chance of someone finding something offensive or off-putting about you. Have clean fingernails, clean shoes and be appropriately dressed. One of my clients always wears cuff links. All his senior people do. It's his thing. It's his standard. So I wear cuff links when I go to see him. I clearly remember working with Mike Moran when he worked for what was then Pharmacia. We had met in a Little Chef in Cumbria. I had, quite frankly, not thought through the implications (more of them later) of visiting vets and farmers in the Lake District. It was in the third vet's surgery with all around me dressed in browns and tweeds and me in my blue suit, white shirt and Armani tie that it really got to me. 'Who's the city slicker then?' said the receptionist just in earshot as Mike and I went in to see the vet. No empathy there then! (Wazzock!) So it's not always about looking like a tailor's dummy, is it?

- Prepare well and think about how you can make a good impression. Don't sit down in someone's office or boardroom until they point to where they want you to sit. I once blew a presentation to a major company in the north of England because I sat in the chairman's favourite seat. Throughout the presentation his whole body language was negative. He wasn't ever really interested. And it was only as we were packing away our flip charts and slides that the marketing manager said: 'I perhaps should have told you the chairman only ever likes to sit in that chair.'

- Listen with rapt attention. People tend to listen with the intention of saying something. Some people even listen with the sole intent of 'topping' your story. Anything you say, they have been at a better or bigger one. Anything you have seen, they have seen a longer and wider one. They know someone more senior. They know someone who took longer, ran faster, went further and so on. If you want people to like you, don't top their stories. Listen with rapt attention. Listen simply so that you can truly understand how they *feel* about what they're saying. Listen so you see things from their point of view. They will like you more and, hell, you might learn something too. More of that later.

- Flatter them and talk about their interests. Most people, in the main, are interested in three things; themselves, their pleasures and their problems.

  So talk about them.

  If you are meeting someone you need to persuade, then flatter him or her by reading up on their subject. When I go to see a potential client I look at their website and print off a page or two. I let them casually see that I have the copy and they always, always, comment on the fact that I've taken the trouble to look at their website. They like that.

  And so do I.

  Say things like: 'That must be really enjoyable', 'How did you feel when that happened?', 'That's quite a story', 'You must be very proud', 'That's fascinating'.

  But be sincere. Be honest. Be genuinely interested in the other person. Don't be a charlatan.
- Feel positive and alive and tell your body. If you're happy, tell your face. If you're not feeling positive, fake it for a day or go home.

I am sitting in a restaurant in Egypt. A man walks in and asks for a table for six people. Picture the scene. The larger tables are taken but there are six tables for four that are not taken (this is not a popular Egyptian restaurant). It is manifestly obvious to me and the guy doing the asking (he had caught my eye) that the waiter will put two tables for four together and make a table for six. But no! He puffs and blows and looks around and says, 'I don't know sir, it's a problem.' A problem! Eventually after *much* puffing and blowing he puts two tables together and we are all happy.

Or are we?

Instead of seeing the opportunity to please a client immediately (and maybe get a good tip) all he sees is the karma disturbed; the work he will have to do to change the table format and then change it back again when we have all gone.

Maybe forever.

A chance missed.

- Remember their name and use their name …

… time for Chapter 4.

How Memory Works and How to Remember People's Names

Thanks to cousin Martin, I was asked to do an engagement for Nike Golf in the summer of 2003. They flew me out to the Dominican Republic, paid for me to work with their team for a day and I played golf with them before I flew home the next day.

Marvellous!

I mention it for three reasons. Firstly, it was very memorable, and later in this chapter I talk about how memory works. Secondly, the client, Johnny Trainor, said to me afterwards, 'That was excellent. Very useful. I was a bit worried it would be "psycho mumbo-jumbo" but it wasn't like that at all. A lot of it is common sense.' And thirdly, it confirmed many of my views about first impressions and the importance of being 'like' other people. If they'd known my golf handicap *before* I spoke to them they would have been in shock! As it was, Mike Smith at Nike wouldn't actually believe my handicap could possibly be higher than 18 so made me play off that. 'You're playing your "hot and cold contrast" with me, Phil [more of that later]. You can't possibly be off 25. I don't know anyone who gets more than one shot a hole. You're off 18.'

So why was the whole thing so memorable? I believe there are three simple criteria for events, people, occasions, indeed, anything, to be remembered and lodged in the subconscious.

Firstly, it needs to be distinctly different or outstanding, which in turn makes it easier to remember. If the essence of selling is to make it easy to buy then the essence of recall is making it easy to remember.

Secondly, it needs to be relevant or of high interest. And thirdly, it needs to be repeated. Remember:

- distinctly different
- relevant
- repeated.

Common sense, isn't it? I recall a recent survey of events in the UK and outside the UK that British people most remembered. The shocking events of September 11 and the untimely death of the Princess of Wales were very clearly the most remembered events. Depending on the age of those asked, the death of JFK in 1963, England winning the World Cup in 1966 and so on, were well remembered. Why? Because they are all distinctly different, they are relevant and of high interest to a wide audience; and, of course, they are endlessly recalled in various ways in the media. I still remember where I was when John F. Kennedy was shot in Dallas. Perhaps you do too, if you have the requisite seniority.

So if you are reading this book because you work in advertising, either in an agency or on the client side responsible for briefing them, ask yourself this question if you want people to remember your campaign: 'Is it distinctly different, is its appeal relevant to our target market and will we repeat it enough to really have the impact we want?'

That, I believe, is how memory works. Humour helps but so does great drama. And often the repetition comes from you, yourself, telling the story to friends and relatives. And who is the person who hears the story the most when you tell the story? *You* of course!

So, remembering people's names? Is there a trick? Well, yes and no. On my courses I often ask, 'Who's bad at remembering people's names?' I can guarantee at least 30% will put their hand up. Often with a glow of pride at just how bad they are!

It's horrocks!

It's just a belief. One delegate once said to me, 'My brother's memory is as bad as mine – we both think we're an only child.' A nice line (and probably an old joke), but the five-step plan to remembering people's names starts with the belief that you can. I'm a big fan of acronyms. This is the first of quite a number of them. But if the acronym is relevant, repeated and distinctly different, it's going to help – isn't it?

The five-step plan to remembering people's names is incorporated in the acronym BLUFF.

B is for Believe you can. Shed all thought of your inability to remember people's names. It's just a belief and most beliefs are just that. It's not true. So stop saying, 'I've always been bad at remembering people's names.' Stop saying, 'I can't remember people's names.' Now.

L is for Listen. Remember we talked about listening with rapt attention? According to my research, most people don't actually hear the other person's name in the first place but carry on chatting anyway. After only 30 seconds it seems too late to say, 'I can't remember your name.' That's because you never got it in the first place! So if you don't catch someone's name, *ask them again for their name.* Do you know, in all the time I've been doing this, if I don't quite catch someone's name and I say, 'I'm sorry, I didn't quite catch your name' no one has ever said, 'I gave you my name once and that's your lot!' They never feel upset or offended. Indeed, they are usually flattered that I want to know their name. So listen, and if you don't hear it, ask them to repeat it. Not rocket science, is it?

I saw an interview recently on TV. Some Chinese scientists were testing a rocket in the Australian outback. It was a prototype and only about 6 feet high but the intention was to eventually produce a rocket that would be able to fly people from one end of the earth to the other. Neat idea. However, the rocket crashed back to earth after only a few hundred yards in the air. Shoving his microphone under the nose of a frustrated scientist, the journalist asked if he was disappointed and deflated. How did he feel? Do you know what he said? 'Well,' he said, as he looked forlornly at the bits of the projectile, 'it *is* rocket science, you know.'

Fantastic!

Got nothing to do with anything, that; but *ask* if you don't hear their name the first time.

U is for Use it. Use their name straight away. Immediately. Bounce it straight back to them. More than once. Not so many times it sounds like you've read a book on how to remember people's names, but these first 60 seconds are critical if you want to remember their name. And you do. Because they'll like it. And they'll like you if you can remember their name. And the more they like you, the better your chance of being persuasive.

F is for Face. Their face. You need to link it with their face even if it's just a simple case of looking at them directly and picturing them as you say their name.

And the final F is for File it or write it down. As soon as you can. Certainly if you are in a meeting and there are several people to work with, write their names down in the positions they are sitting, so at least in the meeting you can glance at your notes. John is sitting next to Joanne, and so on.

After the meeting or encounter, file it. How often, if you do write down their names, do you go back to your notes as soon after the meeting as you can to make notes on the people you have met? The clothes they wore? Their habits, interests, football team, even their birthday? If this person, or these people, you have met are important to you and you need to persuade them over a period of time, gather all the information you can. Gather not only the information on their names but also their interests. If they give you a business card, write on the back (amazing how few people use both sides of a business card, isn't it?) anything you can remember about them. Certainly write down where and when you met them. Finally, write in your diary alongside the appointment the people you met and a one-liner about them.

I was in Marks & Spencer in Harrogate recently. I popped in to buy some shirts and socks. I bumped into an acquaintance. A nice lady – a 'PLU' (People Like Us). 'Hi Sally,' I said. 'How are you?' She paused and then stopped and said hello and how was I and how were the children and it was manifestly obvious she couldn't remember my name. It's okay, isn't it? She doesn't do this for a living. She hasn't been on my course.

But I could tell she was trying to remember my name so I helped her out. 'Chris said to me this morning, "Phil, you need to go to M&S and buy some white shirts. Why don't you pop in now and get me the gift tokens whilst you're there?"'

Sally visibly lightened up. *Now* she had my name and my wife's. And she continued to use my name for the rest of the conversation. So use your own name to help people out and help them remember you. You want to be remembered by the persuadee, don't you? Use your partner's or friend's name in a group, social situation.

Nice.

CHAPTER 5

Relationships – How They Work and How to Work at Them

I want you to imagine your Christmas card list. If you are typical I believe you will find on that list a handful of people who you might describe as 'very close friends'. The kind of friends who, when you call them on the telephone, you don't need to say who you are; you just start talking. No introductions necessary. Close friends that you confide in, turn to, rely on and trust.

Then there's the next 'tranche' of friends. You don't have quite the same close relationship but you get on very well, you see each other socially and are happy to be in their company. And there's more than just a handful of them.

Then there are the people you know and like but don't see a lot of. You might know them but not know their children's names. Friends, yes, but not in the inner circle. And there are more of them. They're all the other people on your list.

It's the triangle of friendships (see Figure 5.1 overleaf). It's how it is. Then there are the people you know but don't really know at all. When you meet you struggle to get past 'ritual and cliché'. 'How are you?' 'Nice weather for ducks.' 'Did you take long to get here?' Blah blah blah. They might not even be on your Christmas card list.

Do you have the same dilemma of most established couples, that once you've started sending and receiving Christmas cards you just keep going ad infinitum? No 'annual review' but rather, 'They always send us one so we'll send them one.' And throughout the year you have developed good relationships with other people but don't bother to send a card. Funny world, isn't it?

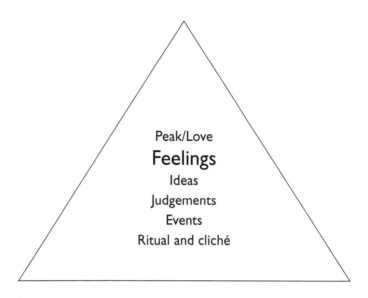

Peak/Love
Feelings
Ideas
Judgements
Events
Ritual and cliché

Figure 5.1 *Triangle of relationships*

But the Christmas card list illustrates how relationships work. The friends at the top of your triangle have worked their way up there because you have common ground, common interests. They're usually (but not exclusively) people like you. But you love them.

Which is nice.

I remember Prince Charles being pilloried by the press when he was asked if he loved the then Lady Diana Spencer. 'Yes,' he said, 'whatever *that* is.' I think he was referring to *love* and not Diana. To be fair to him, love is such an inadequate and insufficient word, isn't it? It's like saying what is between black and white is all grey. One shade. It's like saying that green is the colour that comprehensively describes all the colours you can see from the top of Pen-y-Ghent. Did you know that the Inuit have over a dozen words for 'snow' because it matters to them to be able to describe the difference? When an Inuit comes back home after catching the breakfast and his wife says, 'What's it like out?' there's not much point in replying, 'It looks like snow.' She wants to know what kind of snow so that she can wear the right kind of footwear. 'It's not a stiletto day, darling' would be much more useful.

I love many people but none of them in the same way. Not even women since I threw away the manual in my late teens. I don't even love the immediate members of my family in the same way. But there aren't the easily accessible words to help me communicate all those things. It's nice stuff, love, but it's complicated.

You can discuss feelings (and you don't need to have known each other very long for all this to happen) with people you know well and with people you like. Not just ideas, views and opinions, but how you *feel* about things. It's a deeper relationship when you can talk about how you feel about something. And the word 'feel' is like the word 'love'. If you want to be truly persuasive I want you to consider the word 'feel' as inadequate as the word 'love'. As inadequate as the Inuit would feel if they could only use one word for snow.

Throughout this book I'm going to talk a lot about establishing the other person's need. Their deep need, how they *feel* about what it is you're trying to persuade them to do.

I want to take you onto a higher plane of understanding of how persuasion works so that you become more persuasive. And to do that you need to understand how they *feel*.

Because until you discuss how your persuadee *feels* about a situation, you're stuck in logic, in discussing events and what you've watched on TV. You're just turning features into benefits. At its worst you're just talking ritual and cliché. And people buy emotionally.

The logical part of persuading is the tip of the iceberg we all see, but what really matters is the bit we don't. And I'm sure you know enough about icebergs to know that's the big bit.

When we come to discuss how buying and selling actually work we will see how good planning reduces ritual and cliché and helps speed up the process as well as interesting the buyer. People are far more interested in knowing how much you care, before caring what you know. You have to find out about how your persuadee *feels* about the situation. You need to move up the triangle of relationships and communication so that you get past ritual and cliché and get as high up the triangle as you can, as soon as you can.

THE TISSUE PAPER THEORY

Number 2 son and I were chatting recently about his childhood. I asked him if he could remember me changing his nappies. 'No.' Helping you to ride a bike? 'No.' Teaching you how to swim with your little arm bands on at Coppice Baths? 'No.'

It went on.

I began to think all that love and care and attention and time spent with him were wasted. But they weren't, were they? I saw him as an egg in its fragile shell in a tin box. And every act of kindness, all the things I had done for him and his brothers were like individual layers of tissue paper. And as he grew and eventually went to university, it was the layers of tissue paper in the tin box that would protect him; give him confidence and allow him to feel – and continue to be – strong.

Indeed, when a chicken bursts out of the egg, it isn't an overnight or instant sensation, is it? It has been slowly but surely incubating in the egg until the time is right. And just as the chicken has been nurtured, so too had number 2 son.

And it's the same with your potential client, customer and per-suadee. If you are in the business of building relationships with your clients and customers, remember every act of kindness is another layer of tissue paper. Every time you listen with rapt attention, remember their name and listen to how they feel with genuine empathy: you are adding more tissue paper. And every time you don't do what you say you are going to do, you add an irritant within the layers. Every time you say you think they are wrong you're adding a little broken glass.

Which is not nice.

And if you lie to the person you are trying to persuade you may never, ever recover. Because when trust is broken it sometimes can't be repaired.

After appointing us to create the advertising for his brand, Roger Cooper of Ideal Standard asked me if we would like to do some PR on the appointment. Of course we would. He insisted in no uncertain terms that he needed to approve the press release and whilst I happily agreed, he seemed a little over-zealous in his request. I asked him why and he told me this story.

He had appointed a well-known London agency some years earlier and had insisted on seeing any press release before it went out, and they agreed. Unfortunately for the new agency, the marketing manager at Ideal Standard, Jenny Rustomji, had a son who worked in the press office at *Campaign* magazine. And it was Jenny's son who received a press release from the agency with regard to their appointment by Ideal Standard.

Roger, of course, got to find out about this and was understandably upset because he hadn't seen the release. He then allowed the agency to come up to Hull for the briefing meeting before asking them if they had sent a release without him seeing it. After a number of opportunities for the agency to come clean, he produced the faxed release. He then released the agency.

Trust had been broken irrevocably and that was the end of the relationship.

CONSTRUCTIVE CRITICISM

I speak at seminars and conferences all around the world. I ask delegates if they have ever been offered any 'constructive criticism' and most tell me they have. I ask them which of the two words they pick up on most and how they feel. And everyone tells me the same tale. That they feel they are going to be criticized. Full stop. Nothing constructive about it!

Why is that?

In my experience of offering 'constructive criticism' I found three things happened:

- Firstly, people took it personally and didn't like me.
- Secondly, they disagreed and their knee-jerk reaction was along the lines of 'But … ' and 'The thing is …' or simply, 'You don't understand.'
- Thirdly, they reacted. Not straightaway usually, but afterwards. They spoke to their friends and asked their friends for their view. And guess what? Most times their friend would give them the view they were looking for. They wanted evidence to support their

view and went in search of it. And they could find it with their friends.

As a result there was little or no gain – but a lot lost.

So how *do* you offer 'constructive criticism'? By laying down tissue paper first. By regularly telling people what you think they are good at – with no 'but' and no 'however'.

Then, when you *do* come to offer something a little more critical they are much more likely to take it. You have developed the relationship well enough to give them confidence that you care about them. That you trust them and they trust you.

I found that most times most people know what they are doing wrong and what they need to work on. So say to yourself, 'How can I get the other person to say, "I have a weakness here?" and how can I get them to identify what areas we need to look at?' Often it is as simple as that – ask them where they think they can improve and develop.

But you need to have built up trust. And how do you develop trust apart from always being 100% honest and doing what you say you are going to do?

Rapt attention is the highest form of flattery. It helps develop trust. And good listening is about being curious. My third son, Sebastian, needed some major dental work done over a period of about four years. I would accompany him on all these trips to the hospital and often took along a newspaper to while away the time. Seb and I had been discussing the recently introduced car number plate system. He had asked me how it worked, with two letters first, then two numbers followed by three letters. I didn't know, but as I was sitting with him in the dentist's waiting room at the local hospital I spotted an article in the newspaper that explained how it worked.

'Look Seb, here's the explanation of how the number plates work.' We went through it together and could see how each one of the numbers effectively meant March or September and the following number showed the year. Cleverly, by changing the number for March and September every 10 years the system had 50 years of life in it.

There was only Seb, myself, and the lady receptionist in the waiting room. On hearing our discussion she suddenly chipped in, 'My husband said that system will only last five years.' 'That's interesting,' I said and went on to explain in some detail how the numbering system worked. At the end of the diatribe on my newly found information, do you know what she said?

'Well, like I say, my husband said it'll only last five years.'

She wasn't listening. She had a view, an opinion (her husband's in the event) and looked only for information to support her view. If you want to be persuasive you need to listen with rapt attention. You have to see things from the other person's point of view.

Because, what most people do is just give information without thinking of how the recipient can receive it. I listen to radio traffic announcements. Invariably they tell us what they know, such as an accident at a particular road junction, using their frame of reference and knowledge. Anyone driving through Leeds will hear stuff like 'Chained Bar is very busy, so avoid it.' Where's Chained Bar? Anyone who knows it will probably already know to avoid it in the rush hour. 'A lorry has shed its load of strawberry preserve completely blocking the Woodhead Pass. Drivers are advised to seek an alternative route to avoid the jam.' That's not much good for motorists who don't know that the Woodhead Pass is five miles ahead of them on the A628. And how about suggesting an alternative route?

Still, the 'jam' joke was good. I just had to throw that in.

SAYING THE RIGHT THINGS

Each of those traffic announcements is a classic case of telling people what they want to tell them and not what they need to know. How often do you receive a message on your voicemail where the person leaves you their telephone number so quickly you have to run the message by another couple of times because you couldn't catch it the first time? In hotels, the room service menu is often beautifully designed with some out-of-focus picture of a tomato on the front and wonderful descriptions of the 'bed of lettuce', but what I really want to know is what number to dial to get it. And that's in the small print because the designer doesn't like the look of it. On business cards, why is the contact telephone number often so small that you need to put your glasses on to see it?

Movies on TV take far too long to tell us the names of the technicians such as the sound recordist or wardrobe lady. And then when they do appear, they whizz past so fast you can't read them. That's because they don't expect us to want to know, but they feel obliged to tell us anyway.

I hate to see channel brand names on satellite television. I want to watch the programme without a constant reminder that I'm watching the Geographic Channel or the Paramount Channel or the Adult Channel. (*Note to editor: delete that last one.*) (*No – ed.*) I mean, why *do* Channel 5 bosses insist on having their logo on screen all the time? It's not for our enjoyment, is it? They're telling us what they want to tell us and not what we want to know.

How often do *you* tell people what *you* want to tell them and *not* what *they* want to know? With the exception of filing your tax return, it's bad form.

So what can you say that is persuasive and will help you build a relationship so that you can achieve what you wish?

Well, here are the Top Ten Things to Start Saying to ensure you will be more liked by more people and, as a result, become more persuasive and influential:

I 'I'll tell you what I like about you'

This is, I believe, the most persuasive thing you can ever say to anyone; but it has a flaw.

You need to know what you are going to say next. If you say it and the person you are talking to says, 'What's that?' and you reply, 'I don't know, I read it in a book', it doesn't work.

You need to know what you are going to say next. You also need to make sure you don't say something like, 'How do you ignore all those horrible things that people say about you behind your back?' Not good.

As well as being flattering, you need to be absolutely sincere, honest and genuine. Everyone wants to know what you like about them. They will like you more and if they like you more it will be easier to persuade them. It helps build a real relationship. But you have to be honest in your compliment.

2 'I'll tell you what I think you're really good at'

'Lying your way out of any tricky situation' is another example of how not to complete this very promising opening line. In effect, it's an extension of number 1 and is great to use with work colleagues. Again, you have to be sincere. If you have a colleague you don't get on with as well as you might, talk to their best friend about what you admire about them and what you think they're really good at. Be honest, sincere and genuine.

What does their buddy do? Goes and tells their friend, of course. And they, in turn, will like you more and that helps you build that relationship.

I believe these first two things to start saying are at the heart of being a great company. The view that 'people are your greatest asset' really needs a caveat. Your *best* people are definitely your greatest asset; but what about the ones you have question marks about? The fact is, all the successful companies I see have got, in the main, the right people – and in the right jobs. If you have that *and* you develop them *and* you keep telling them what they're good at, you usually have a growing company with a happy team of people on board too. And isn't that what we all want?

So:

- tell people what you think they're really good at;
- be sincere;
- be honest;
- be genuine;
- be selfless; and
- be generous – tell their friends too.

3 'Why do you ask?'

We had a Bosnian cleaning lady at home at a time when my eldest son was in Canada on a year out after finishing university. My conversations with Senka tended to be based on, 'Hello, Senka. How are you?' 'I'm fine thanks, Phil. How are you?' I would then make myself a coffee and go back to my office. One day she asked how David was in Canada. 'Fine, thanks, Senka.' 'Is he safe?' she said. 'Yes, he's safe.' 'Everything's OK with him; there are no problems?' As I replied in the affirmative it was only after she asked her fifth question about my son's well-being that I then said, 'Why do you ask?'

'Because,' she began, clearly holding back tears, 'my son has just gone to America and it's the first time he's been away from home and I'm really worried about him.'

She wasn't concerned about my son at all, was she? She was concerned about hers. Naturally, I sacked her on the spot. Only kidding. So if someone is asking you the same question in more than one way, ask them why. Then you get to know their concerns, which in turn leads to greater understanding and greater empathy – and your ability to persuade them.

4 'How was yours?'

I worked in an office environment for many years. On Monday mornings people would pop their head round the door. 'Morning, Phil. Had a good weekend?' On returning from holiday at the end of August there would be a clutch of people also returning from holiday. 'Hi, Phil. Had a good holiday?' I would always reply to these questions 'Great, thanks. How was yours?'

Do you know, in all the time I did this no one ever said, 'Hang on. I asked about your holiday.' Or 'No, tell me about your weekend.' The point is that people are usually not interested in your weekend, your holiday or your well-being. They're interested in theirs. So get them to do the talking. It builds up their perception of the amount you care; and that builds empathy. It means they like you more, which in turn gives you a better opportunity to persuade.

5 'I can see it from your point of view'

And this too has a flaw. A key focus of this book is to see things from the other person's point of view. Arguably it's the definition of empathy. If you say, 'I agree with you', you lose your position. But if you say, 'I don't agree' you lose empathy. So to say, 'I can see it from your point of view' has them thinking that you understand their position. But, as I say, it has a flaw.

The flaw is that if 'I can see it from your point of view' is quickly followed by 'but …', you may as well not bother. The secret is to follow it *always* with '… and …'. If you do always use 'and' you will find yourself being more conciliatory and persuasive. You can still make the point you want to make *and* the other person will like you more *and* you will continue to build empathy.

Indeed, avoid the word 'but' whenever you can – it's inherently confrontational.

It is just after ten o' clock in the morning on a damp and wintry day in Newcastle upon Tyne. My son Daniel, sporting an overcoat, a fashionably tied scarf and a trilby – yes, a trilby hat – is about to leave his upstairs flat as he has a lecture at eleven. As he descends the stairs the doorbell sounds, so he answers the door with hat on and a rucksack over his left shoulder. The man at the door – a slight man in his sixties – is dressed for the cold of the north-east of England in February and has a letter in his hand, an identity badge around his neck and, yes, a trilby on his head.

He shows Daniel the letter for a 'Mrs P. Rowson', at which point Daniel professes his admiration for the accomplished way in which his male flatmate has apparently been concealing his true gender. The older man laughs as Daniel tries to remain cool whilst transfixed by the 'TV Licensing Authority' stamp at the top of the letter, more than a little conscious of the fact that Daniel, Peter (the aforementioned 'Mrs' Rowson) and their three other flatmates have spent the last six months 'getting round' to buying a TV licence. Predictably enough, the man from the Authority enquires as to whether or not they have a television and Daniel replies whimsically, 'As it happens we don't have a television'. This is then how it goes:

'Well, I'm sure you won't mind if I pop in to verify that fact.'

'You know, I'd actually prefer it if you didn't, as it happens. Now is not a terribly good time.'

(Dan is doing his best to effect what he later that day described to me as 'a rather charming, urbane air'.)

'Well,' says our trilbied friend with a wry smile, 'it doesn't quite work like that. Basically if you refuse me entry now, then tomorrow the enforcers come round and *they* check.'

'Well,' replies Daniel, 'not that we have a TV anyway, but if we *were* to have one I'm sure there wouldn't be any evidence of one tomorrow.'

'No, I don't suppose there would,' he, in turn, replied, 'but we already have evidence that you have a TV and I'm afraid that would mean you have to pay the fine of £1,500.'

£1,500!

'So what would be the options available to me and my flatmates in this hypothetical situation if we were to have a TV?'

'Well, you either let me in now and I see your hypothetical TV and give you a bill for £1,500, or the enforcer comes round tomorrow and, regardless of whether there is a TV or not, he hands over the fine for £1,500.'

This is not looking good.

'Nice hat,' says Dan.

'Thanks. I've had it for ages. They seem to be coming back in fashion amongst students.'

'Very much so. Most of my friends have them. They keep you warm and they are considered to be pretty cool.'

(I am not making this up.)

Daniel senses a pause in the conversation but notices the man is smiling.

'You must know of another way – what can I do? I'm a poor student – I'm sure you don't enjoy giving these fines out. With all your knowledge of how the TV licensing authorities work, I'm sure you know of another option ...'

The man on the doorstep smiles and looks at Daniel, who now delivers line number six:

'If you were me, a poor student – who doesn't mean anyone any harm – in my situation – what would you do?'

He paused and said, 'I'd ring the TV licensing authorities right now and buy a TV licence over the phone. The licence costs just £110 so you'll be saving yourself £1,390. I'd put down on my form that I arrived after you had bought the licence ...'

Daniel couldn't help but laugh. 'That's a fabulous idea! I've got my cash card in my pocket – just let me run upstairs and get my phone.'

'No need,' he replied, reaching into his bag. 'You can use mine.'

They chat some more about the numerous benefits of hats and Daniel listens with rapt attention as he extolled the virtues of the trilby.

> Daniel finishes his conversation with the TV licence people, hands back the mobile phone and the man shakes him by the hand and tells the young student the experience has been 'a real pleasure'.

Hence 'right thing to say' number six:

6 'If you were me, what would you do right now?'

I have absolutely not made up a word of that. Frankly, I don't have the wit or imagination to do so. And neither, bless him, does Dan. He told the man what he liked about him. He could not see a way out of it and as a last resort appealed not only to the guy's better nature but also for a resolution *he* might just have.

It's a great line to use when someone is extremely angry with you, too. One of the most effective things about the line is that it almost forces the other person to see things from your perspective – no need to tell them what you're thinking, feeling or going through. Once you hear those words 'what would *you* do …' it sets off a train of thought that would perhaps otherwise be difficult to instigate. You get to know just how much they want from you. It allows you to understand and then manage expectations. I've used it when I worked in advertising, when we had made an error and the client was unhappy. It's a great way of finding out not just how bad things are, but often finding a solution you, yourself, are struggling to find.

Real life is always funnier than gags, isn't it?

7 'I wonder if you could help me?'

We all want to feel important. We all want other people to see us as knowledgeable. So starting a request for information with, 'I wonder if you can help me?' will invariably produce the answer, 'Yes.'

Because you are making the other person feel important. You are also, in a small way, making them feel obliged to help you because they have said they would. (More of that in Chapter 20.)

8 'I understand how you feel'

Earlier in this chapter, we talked about the importance of appreciating how people 'feel' about your idea, product, service or excuse. Particularly if someone has an objection, it is not quite enough to say that you understand their position. It's barely adequate to say that you acknowledge their point of view.

You need them to feel that you understand how they feel. So use this one. Tell people you understand how they *feel*. But make sure you do. Don't say you do if you don't.

And don't forget to tell the people you love the most that you know how *they* feel too.

9 'Is there more?'

When people confront us with objections or news that we don't like, it's so easy to fight back against the objections. That's because we want to provide solutions (more on that later); but we can find them too soon and think we have encountered the objection when the real issue is still left unresolved. We need to find the bottom of the barrel. We need to understand how someone feels about *the whole issue*. So before you start to offer solutions, ask if there's more. Because if there is, then that's what you need to know.

10 'Thank you for your faith in me'

In Chapter 11 we look at the importance of rapport and empathy in negotiation. We also examine how important it is to understand that, typically, after you have done your persuading, your buyer is left with a concern or two. Will he 'manage' what you have persuaded him to do or buy? Has he done the right thing? So if someone has put their faith in you, it is a great way of empathizing by saying, 'I know you have concerns – I will still be with you.'

Finally, a great thing to *do* rather than say – and it could be one of the best things you ever do.

Ask a friend to tell you the most irritating thing about you.

It could turn out to be the biggest step you make on being persuasive and living your life in a more influential manner. We all have 'things' about us that other people find irritating, or even downright rude and off-putting. I watched a TV programme the other night about a football hooligan fresh out of prison. He had a well-meaning mentor who was trying to help him with the transition from prison to civilian life. Trouble was, the lad couldn't look anyone in the eye. I'm sure I wasn't alone in finding this very off-putting. But probably no one had told him. And his chances of getting a job would have been greatly enhanced by looking interviewers in the eye rather than giving the consistent impression of a shady character who wasn't to be trusted.

The truth is that we all have traits that others don't like. So ask the friends you trust the most to tell you what yours are. Ask them to be sincere, honest, genuine and blunt. Ask them what traits you have that they find irritating. Then resist the temptation to punch their lights out. That's not a good trait either.

Then try to stop doing all the things that annoy them.

And, really finally, a word about the French.

We Brits are more conservative than the French. In some respects it's easier for us to be slower to intimacy. But the French have things more organized, as I see it. The whole 'air-kiss-when-you-meet' is interesting. If I understand it correctly (and depending on a lot of factors such as age, who is introducing you, dress, their accents – I could go on ...), they start with the 'double air-kiss' at 'ritual and cliché' but there's no touching. As they get to know each other a little better, the 'double air-kiss' includes touching cheeks; and as they move up the triangle of relationships the 'double air-kiss' includes actually kissing the cheeks. Then it gets even more interesting. Because as they move from 'feelings' to 'peak' the kisses on the cheeks get nearer to the mouth until, hey presto, they are kissing on the lips.

On top of that there's the tu/vous dilemma, where 'tu' is the familiar form of 'you' and 'vous' is the more formal version. It seems to me that most people who work together call each other 'tu' unless someone is older or unknown to them, in which case it's 'vous'. If people think you are less senior they 'vous' you, and if you have been 'tu-tu'd' *until* then it's a real insult. So how do you decide to graduate from one to the other?

To be fair, they also have more words than us for kissing – but even that is wholly inadequate, don't you think? As we said earlier in the chapter, 'love' has so much meaning and to say you 'kissed' someone can mean very different things depending on how you interpret it. And how do you adjust what the Italians call the 'vital bubble' around you when we are less comfortable with having our faces and bodies nearer to others?

We all have an 'aura' around us, and we are only comfortable with certain people (i.e. those close to us) 'entering' that 'aura'. Step into a stranger's and you reduce your chance of being persuasive.

The study of the distances between us, incidentally, is called proxemics. Isn't that a great word?

Let's get back to the Principles of Persuasion.

PART 2

How Persuasion and Influence Work

CHAPTER 6

The Principles of Persuasion

There's an untrue but nonetheless widely held view that selling and being persuasive is about talking. That it's about being 'slick.' That the 'gift of the gab' is the key element to being persuasive.

Horrocks.

Over the years I have asked many, many professional buyers what the key elements are for being persuasive. In other words, *who* do they buy from and what do they *like* about good persuaders? This is the summary of that research. These are the key attributes of a good persuader from the buyer's perspective:

- They are honest. (And this is first because *they* put it first when I ask people to rank the importance of what they have said.)
- They want to understand my business; they want to understand my needs; they want to understand my frustrations.
- They genuinely care. They sell for my reasons and not just theirs.
- I learn from them.
- They seem to appreciate how difficult my job is.
- They want to be my partner and therefore I want them as mine.
- They remain interested after the sale and want to know how things are. They don't just go away after they have sold to me.

The following, I believe, are the first three principles of persuasion.

ESTABLISH THE OTHER PERSON'S EMOTIONAL NEEDS

It's an old and well-used expression that 'people buy people first'. I offer no apology for repeating it here. It's as true today in the fast-living world of e-mail, mobile phones and videoconferencing as it's ever been. Our friend Ecclesiastes probably said it. And remember, people buy people who are like them or, at least, act and behave like them and have similar values. People will like you if you behave like them and mirror their body language.

The more people talk, the more they like you. Have you ever heard anyone say, 'He's a regular guy, he's quite nice but he just listens too much'?

Effective persuaders listen more than they talk.

So your persuadee must truly believe in you. He or she must believe that you are more concerned with their situation than you are about simply getting your own way. He or she must believe that you will do whatever is necessary that's in his or her interests. Without trust and the belief that you will do what you say you are going to do, all the benefits, added value or discounts don't mean a thing. So you have to be sincerely interested in their situation to be a top persuader.

And you have to be honest.

People buy emotionally and justify logically. Everything you have ever bought has been bought emotionally. The clothes you are wearing right now, the watch on your wrist, the car you drive, the house you live in, the restaurant you last had a meal in, the brands you have in your pantry and fridge. Everything. Why else would there be over 20 brands of bottled water in the average UK supermarket? You can't *really* tell the difference, can you?

It's what my wife calls 'marketing horrocks'. In later chapters we explore the importance of understanding the psychology of emotional buying. For now, the first principle of persuasion is that you need to establish not just the other person's logical, stated needs, but their emotional needs too. You typically only do that when you have a relationship. And you only have a relationship when they like you.

Bit of an effort, isn't it? But being professional is an effort, isn't it? It's not what you do, it's the way that you do it. And that's what gets results. As Bananarama once put it.

> I'm sitting on an aeroplane flying from Rome to Manchester. The pilot is speaking in that way they're trained to talk: it's both patronizing and paternal, and he asks us if we can 'pop' down our newspapers while our flight attendants take us through the safety procedures. Doctors do it too. They ask you to 'pop' your clothes off as though it'll reduce the pain and embarrassment of doing so. I don't think they quite get that it's not the taking off the clothes that's embarrassing; it's standing there with shirt and tie but no pants on that's the embarrassing bit. But language is important and it's not *what you say* but *how you say it* that often conveys that you care.

THE ESSENCE OF SELLING IS TO MAKE IT EASY FOR PEOPLE TO BUY

The rest of this book explores and develops this principle. As a good persuader you need to be constantly saying to yourself: 'Can I make this easier?' Most of my clients' products and services solve *problems* the buyer has, so the better you understand and have true empathy with their problem, the better the chance of being persuasive – and the better you ease the buyer's pain, the better for you.

More of that later, too.

Why are instructions on the back of ready-meals in such small type? The older people – the ones with the money – are losing their eyesight and if the essence of selling is to make it easier for people to buy, so making it easier for things to be *used* will increase the likelihood of the product being bought again. Can anyone tell me why for years you had to open a carton of milk at the wrong end in order to read the words 'open other end'? Even great food manufacturers like Heinz aren't altogether explicit with their instructions on sauce bottles. *'Shake well before use'* could mean three or four days before pouring!

I love how we're presented with attractive items to buy whilst standing at the supermarket checkout. Isn't that a superb example of making it easy for people to buy? You have time to kill, a desire to do something and an open basket. But I feel many retailers miss opportunities of this nature. When I'm buying shoes, what do I look at when the assistant has gone to get me my size to try on? Should I not be looking at other items that I might be interested in?

I'm surprised that dentists' waiting rooms only having old copies of *Horse and Hound* or *Cosmopolitan*. My mood and circumstance are such that I'm interested in dental care, and yet so few dentists I see make it easy for me to buy toothbrushes, toothpaste, dental floss and so on. Sunglasses at opticians, crèches in menswear departments so that Dad can look at a leisurely pace and find it easy to buy.

Of course, many do it well. But the 'Do you want fries with that?' mentality doesn't permeate all the way through shop assistants in dry cleaners (stay crease), video stores (popcorn), lawnmowers (hedge trimmers) and so on.

But, as with all broad brush strokes, there is another side to the story. I know a number of women who hold the view that stores that sell bras deliberately confuse. Their theory is that there is little information about 'what does what' so that you take more bras into the changing room and, as a result, buy more.

Maybe.

I am walking up a street in a local town. I have had a good meeting with a client, I have plenty of money in my parking meter and it is a lovely sunny day. I pass a menswear shop and see a Sand suit in the window.

(Some months ago I had a speaking engagement with First Direct. Two attractive young women approached me after my session and gave me positive and encouraging feedback. They then said, their colleagues at a previous talk I had done 'were right about the suit'. I asked them to explain and they told me that their colleagues thought that I wore a lovely suit. I became known, apparently, as 'the guy with the suit'. Now that was a Sand suit. So I like Sand suits. Young, intelligent, attractive women think I look good in a Sand suit so as I walk by the shop and see a Sand suit in the window, I check I have my credit cards with me and walk into the shop. Shoppers don't come hotter than this.)

I approach the salesman – who, it turns out, is the owner of the shop. He asks if he can help me and I say that I notice he has a 'Sand' suit in the window. Does he have the same suit in dark blue or black in my size, I ask. Yes he does, and he picks the suit off the hook and lays it down on the counter.

This is encouraging. But he then goes on to do something amazing. He says, 'I've nothing against Sand but ...' and goes on to tell me how the cut and design of another brand is better. He tells me what he knows about this other brand, where they are made and the quality of the fabric. He takes a suit off the hook and lays it on top of 'my' suit.

'My' suit!

Why? I want to buy the Sand suit! Why doesn't he ask me questions? Why doesn't he ask me what I like about Sand suits and why I *feel* that way? Why does he want to *educate* me? Why doesn't he make it easy to buy?

I leave the shop and am now looking for a retailer who not only sells Sand suits but will let me buy one; a retailer who doesn't simply want to tell me what he knows.

Advice? Make it as easy as possible for your buyer to buy. There are no objections, there are 'issues to address'. You don't have a 'cheaper model', you have one that 'might fit your budget' and is 'excellent value for money'. Don't ask people to sign a contract, ask them if they would like to 'autograph the paperwork'.

And so on.

PEOPLE DON'T WANT CHEAP BRANDS BUT THEY DO WANT BRANDS CHEAP

Or, to put another way, 'sell value and not price'.

People want value. The word 'cheap' doesn't necessarily mean that, does it? It carries with it baggage that says 'poor quality'. So what is 'value'? Value is quality divided by price. And by quality I mean *perceived* quality.

Remember Alan Fish and the aspirin for different parts of the body? I want you to imagine a market stall. At one end of the market stall there are bananas at 20p per lb. At the other end of the stall there are bananas at 30p per lb. A lady asks why some bananas are 20p and some are 30p per lb. Pointing at each of the bananas in turn the stall-holder replies, 'These bananas are for people who want to pay 20p per lb and these are for people who want to pay 30p per lb.'

And isn't that the case sometimes? In fashion, men and women often don't want to pay less than £300 or so for a suit because they believe they need to pay that much for the quality they desire. It doesn't matter whether that's true or not; it's their belief. Because our advertising agency was in Leeds, there was a belief held by many potential clients that we couldn't be as creative as agencies in London. On one occasion a client was interested in giving us a design project but told us that we were not expensive enough. He felt he had to pay more!

But how does value manifest itself as you pay more and more? The Price Perception Curve (Figure 6.1) shows how it works. As you pay more you get *less* in tangible benefits. A car at £20,000 is arguably twice as good as one at £10,000 – but a car at £100,000 can't possibly be 10 times better, can it? Well, logically it can't but we don't buy logically.

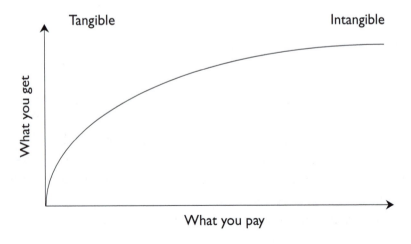

Figure 6.1 *Price perception curve*

The benefits just become more intangible. They become more about image, mystique, ego and perceived benefit. I love the admission by Stella Artois that it is 'Reassuringly Expensive'.

Get in!

I am sitting in a hotel in Richmond, Surrey. Well, I say hotel. It's a pub. An old and dirty pub with no hot water and no marmalade. The bar stools that in the evening light were not noticeable are, in the cold light of day, worse than shabby. The owner doesn't care and I won't be coming back.

But it's cheap.

Only last week I stayed at the Pennyhill Park Hotel and Country Club, also in Surrey. Hotels don't get much better. The manager, Danny Peccorelli, runs a fine ship with assiduous attention to detail.

And it's expensive.

Quite rightly.

But, at £150 a night, is it 10 times better than the one down the road? Well, yes and no. Looking at it logically, each hotel provided me with a clean bed, a cold beer, a hot snack and an early morning call. But I'd rather pay the premium. The benefits are there but they are *intangible*. It's about attitude and attention to detail. It's about care.

Flowers show you care. If you are responsible for an office, have fresh flowers in reception. It says a lot about the organization.

If you are responsible for a retail outlet or a hotel, make sure every visitor or guest is acknowledged as soon as possible. A wait seems shorter when your customer knows that you are aware of them. And a wait is easier when there's someone to talk to.

In Harrods I notice that the guards and the guys who shift boxes from A to B wear aftershave. BO can be so off-putting, and a little thing like that shows you are in an establishment where somebody thought about it. Somebody cares.

First impressions, remember? They stay with us.

It is a Saturday. My youngest son, Seb, is going to Africa tomorrow. He wants to look after monkeys and work with wild animals. He has bought a digital camera on the Internet after painstaking research, but it hasn't arrived in the post and isn't going to be here before he flies. So, we go into town. I have agreed to buy him a camera and I will have the one that is somewhere in the postal system.

We find a specialist camera retailer and ask the owner of the shop if he has this particular camera. The good news is that he does, the bad news is that it is £70 more expensive than buying on the web. Seb shows him the printout from the website and he asks the guy if he can match the price.

Not only is the answer 'no', but we get an education on the costs of running a high street shop versus selling on the web.

I am standing back and watching. Why doesn't the retailer put the camera in his hand and allow him to handle it? Why doesn't he ask him *when* he needs it? Why doesn't he talk about the *intangible* benefits such as the fact that the shopkeeper can offer advice and feedback? Such as the fact that the web supplier cannot supply before midnight! My son is willing to pay the premium (he's going away tomorrow) but needs to have the premium justified by intangible benefits.

He needs to establish my son's emotional needs. He needs to make it easy for him to buy. He needs to talk emotional value and not just price.

We leave the store.

We conducted some research for Tetley's beer some years ago. We carried out exit interviews at pubs that were in highly affluent suburban areas and compared them with those in what were known as 'town drinking houses'. One of the key questions was, 'Do you know the price of a pint of beer?' This question was only asked of those people who'd actually bought a pint of beer and the results were interesting.

Less than 50% of the people coming out of the affluent pubs said they knew the price of a pint of beer, but the majority of them were wrong when we asked them for the amount. Whereas 90% of the customers of the town drinking houses said they knew the price and, surprise, surprise, the vast majority of them were right when they told us the price they paid. You're buying much more than a pint, aren't you? Indeed, for some men in particular, ignoring the price tag is an act of virility. I remember the movie *The Yellow Rolls-Royce* when, in Genoa, the American gangster Paolo Maltese is interested in buying the car to tour Italy, and enquired at the Rolls-Royce dealer if he could buy 'the yellow Royce-Rolls', as that's what the young lady on his arm wanted. The salesman was busy correcting him when he said, 'If my hunny bun wants a yellow Royce-Rolls, my hunny bun gets a yellow Royce-Rolls.'

Price was never going to be an issue, was it?

Another piece of research was the '625 Test' to which I made reference in Chapter 2. We recruited people on the basis that they had a very strong preference for either John Smith's bitter or Tetley's bitter. They were only asked to participate if they were bigots who would only drink one rather than the other. We gave each individual two half glasses of beer and asked them to tell us which one they preferred, i.e. which one was their favoured brand. Glass 'A' on the left was Tetley's and glass 'B' on the right was John Smith's. We then repeated the same thing three times. So, on four occasions they were given two beers and asked to take a sip from glass 'A' and glass 'B', and report on which they preferred. Unknown to them 'A' was *always* Tetley and 'B' was *always* John Smith's. It was called the '625 Test' because they had a one in two chance (i.e. 0.5) each time of telling us which was their favoured brand. ($0.5 \times 0.5 \times 0.5 \times 0.5 = .0625$).

Over 90% of these men and women who expressed a strong preference for a particular brand did not know one from the other.

Fact.

Did it then change their mind about the brand they didn't like after we told them the results? Not usually.

And what about Mont Blanc? I'm talking fountain pen not mountain. They're expensive, aren't they? More of them later.

If you're going to be expensive you need to be consistently expensive. So we need to sell *emotional* value to the buyer, not price. We need to persuade on the emotional footing of value for that individual and not the logical footing of price. In selling, price is often the first objection raised. So later we look at ways of overcoming that by getting away from price and into the emotional value to the other person.

I am sitting with my family in a beautiful bay on the south-east coast of Spain. We have been away from Britain for three and a half weeks and are just about as relaxed as relaxed can be. We have had a pleasant day in our villa by the pool, and have meandered down to the local bar for a drink and to watch people come and go.

We are sitting at a little table, sipping our drinks and watching the holidaymakers, when an English couple come to sit at the table next to us. It is obvious that they have just flown in. Their stress levels are high and it's only the contrast with how we feel that makes us realize that this is the case. 'Mum' is tense. She is breathing heavily but trying to read a book. Her 12-year-old is anxious to get on with the holiday and wants to play with the ball.

'Mum' turns on him and says, 'I've told you – just chill!'

She says it with the kind of fury reserved for a woman at the end of her tether. The fact is, it takes time to unwind and adjust to sun, sand and sea. In the same way it takes us time to absorb new things. When we walk into a retail outlet it's a bit like entering a decompression zone. We need time to adjust to our surroundings; we need a soft landing and time for our subconscious mind to catch up with our conscious mind.

Mood and circumstance are important in persuasion.

QTV in post offices just doesn't do it for me. You're in the queue and getting frustrated and you have other things to do. The circumstances appear to be right to give us a new message but our mood is all wrong. Sitting at the breakfast table is a great time to read the back of a cereal box. In the toilet, quite frankly, we'll read anything – including the back of a shampoo bottle if that's all that's available.

FORMS OF MOTIVATION

Let's finish this chapter on the principles of persuasion by touching on the issue of motivation. People are usually driven or drawn. People are driven *away from* what they don't want or drawn *to* what they do want. And often they don't know why they are doing it. Some people buy things they don't need with money they haven't got to impress people they don't like!

People don't always need reasons to be persuaded. They just need emotional satisfaction. Some people buy because they think they are going to save time. To paraphrase The Eagles: 'You spend all your time making money and you spend all your money making time.' Sometimes people buy because they want to be recognized. Why else would the market for personalized number plates be so lucrative? Sometimes there is a real personal pride of ownership, and sometimes it's a case of keeping up with the Joneses.

It could be argued that people do things and are persuaded to buy things for one of four reasons. What 'FORM' does your motivation take?

F is for Fun
Sometimes you do things just for the hell of it. Often you buy something on impulse because you like it and it feels good.

O is for Obligation
Often we do things because we feel obliged. (More of that when we look at the psychological *reasons* for how and why people buy.)

R is for Rejection or Running Away
Sometimes we buy because we fear what will happen if we don't buy. For example, security products that allows us to *feel* that we are safe from burglars. Sometimes we are persuaded because we want to avoid the pain of criticism.

I was canoeing in the Canadian Rockies with my eldest son, and the leader in the six man Canadian canoe was chatting to me about motivation. He was awaiting his moment, unbeknown to me, and then said just at the right time, 'See that sign over there?'; and sure enough there was a huge sign saying 'Waterfall 1 kilometre. Please leave the river at the next bank.' He asked me if we had seen the waterfall. And we had – huge it was – and certain death awaited anyone who attempted to go over it in a canoe. 'Okay,' he said. 'The current's strong and we all gotta paddle like crazy to make sure we make the bank on the right.' We looked round and all paddled like never before. He tapped me on the shoulder and shouted above the din of the fast running water, *'That's* motivation!'

Well, at least it's one form of motivation. It's not a healthy one to rely on in a successful, growing company. Indeed there's a strong case for spending time and effort making sure you don't *demotivate* people by using 'Rejection' inadvertently.

M, of course, is for Money

Making it or saving it. Big motivator this one, but so often not as important as we think it is.

When we handled the Brentfords retail account I came up with the idea of testing the effectiveness of advertising by using it for certain stores, but not for others. Given that the size of stores, average weekly sales and type of area were 'graded' anyway, we would match stores against others and we would be able to see how useful the advertising was. The weather would be roughly the same, as would general economic conditions, so we anticipated that stores *with* advertising would outperform those *without*. But a handful of stores always bucked the trend. And why? Because there was a financial incentive for the managers to beat targets? Not really. What we discovered was that the managers *without* advertising just wanted to outperform the stores *with*, to show they were better managers; that good management was more important than a good ad! Money? They told me (it took a while to unearth what was happening) that it was for the fun of it ...

Right now it's time for the NAIL.

CHAPTER 7

The NAIL

I want you to imagine a dog on a house porch; an American clapboard-style house porch with granny sitting in her rocking chair taking in the evening air. She lives next to the gasworks but she's used to it. The dog is whining slowly and softly because he's in a little pain.

The reason that he's experiencing a little pain is because he's lying on a nail. A large nail. But he doesn't move. He just keeps whining.

Doesn't it feel like that for you sometimes when you are trying to persuade someone to your point of view and they don't seem to get it? Why don't they buy into your idea, product, service or excuse?

Same reason as the dog doesn't move. The nail doesn't hurt enough.

There isn't enough motivation to move. So you have to build the need by either amplifying the pain or explaining the benefits of moving to a different part of the porch. In certain zoos there are temperature controls underground inside the animal enclosures, near to the public viewing areas. Now, if you go to a zoo you want to see the lions, tigers and jaguars and you want to be as near as possible without being in any danger. So on hot days, the zoo keeper reduces the temperature under the ground nearest to the visitors so the animals lie nearest to the public viewing areas. On cold days, guess what? That's right, they turn the temperature right up so the animals want to be near to where the public are.

And so it is with persuasion. We need to establish the motivation and mindset of the other person – in this case, the animals. You don't get very far prodding half a ton of lion with a stick and, in today's business environment, you don't get far just with a big stick either.

We need to amplify the dog's pain or point out how much better it would be somewhere else. So the NAIL is an acronym and the N stands for Need.

N IS FOR NEED

Remember the guy looking for a Boss suit? His need was for a Boss suit because his belief was that it was an excellent brand and that was the brand for him. If you asked him *why* he liked that brand he would no doubt give you logical reasons. Previous experience of the brand, a view on the cut and design being right for him and so on.

But the major issue is, that he had an emotional attachment and belief. His need was for a Boss suit or something very similar, and our retailer lost any chance of selling him a suit when he didn't identify the buyer's need and belief system. Similarly my retail friend didn't establish my view on the Sand suit.

If you have ever bought a house you will have no doubt considered three key factors:

- What is it?
- Where is it?
- How much?

They *appear* to be the needs. The basic needs.

But it's an emotional decision, isn't it? If you can think about when you bought your house, you became emotional about it. Indeed, if you are honest with yourself you will acknowledge that you don't really know why you fell in love with it.

When we first viewed the house we currently live in (and have done since 1987) my wife glanced over her shoulder at me as we walked in the front door with a look that only women can do, and said with her eyes: 'Say nothing – we're buying this house. This is ours.' We had only seen the view from the front and the hall.

Do you know, women have more facial muscles than men have? Men are just not as able to be as expressive as women!

Remember Gerald Zaltman's 95:5 rule? He declared that most of the time we don't know what we're doing. We justify logically but we buy emotionally. And the needs of the other person you are trying to persuade often need 'teasing' out of them because initially they talk about the logical issues, and they themselves don't really know what they want. That's why we buy the house that cost twenty grand more than we really wanted to pay, or why we have a shiny new two-seater Cabriolet on the drive and a baby on the way.

Here are five things you need to know about customers.

1   People don't always know what they want.
2   They know what they like when they see it.
3   They know whose money it is.
4   Often what they think is important in the buying process is different to what you think should be important.
5   Men and women are very different.

I was in the John Lewis department store in Nottingham recently. I got chatting to the guy responsible for selling laptops and PCs. He told me that earlier that morning, a female student at the University of Nottingham had called in. She said she was looking for a laptop.

'Nothing fancy really – just something that does Word. I don't need Excel or PowerPoint or anything. Just something that will allow me to do my essays.'

Understandably he made an assumption that price was important and showed her the bottom of the range laptop at £800. As she was looking at it her eye was caught by another laptop at £1,800.

'Does that one do Word?' she said as she surreptitiously glanced over at the more attractive laptop.

'Certainly,' the salesman replied.

'I'll have that then.'

I couldn't make that up, could I?!

What *appeared* to be her need was not the full story. Perhaps she thought that a laptop would say something about her to her friends. Perhaps she just liked the look of it. Perhaps she wanted to show the salesman she could buy anything she wanted. Perhaps she herself didn't know. Perhaps she never will.

She bought emotionally. And what appeared to be her need was not the full story.

I want you to imagine that you are selling boxes of widgets. You have come to the point in your presentation where you have asked the buyer for a commitment to buy.

You have an ongoing relationship with this buyer and wish to build the relationship further. As you ask for the commitment to buy, the buyer says to you: 'Could I take delivery by the first of the month?'

Now, you *can* ensure delivery by the first of the month. Do you always say 'Yes' and close the sale?

It would be easy to. But I believe it's best not to. I believe that the best thing to do in those circumstances is to say: 'Is taking delivery by the first of the month important to you?'

There are then basically two options. If it isn't terribly important for him to have delivery by the first of the month, you can establish the range of dates when it would be ideal for him, and get back to him as soon as you wish.

Nothing lost.

But let's say that having delivery by the first of the month is crucial. Let's suppose that not having delivery by the first of the month would cause headaches for him; let's suppose he would have a whole bunch of unhappy customers if you couldn't organize delivery by the first of the month.

Now you know his need. And, knowing his need you can build the relationship and/or sell more widgets. You could tell him that you will do everything in your power to ensure delivery but there will be some effort in it. It will involve more than just putting it down on your order pad. It will involve him being indebted to you for the effort you have expended to establish delivery by the first of the month. Or, of course, you could say something like: 'Delivery by the first of the month isn't straightforward. At the moment you are only taking 200 boxes of widgets. If you were to take a full lorry load of 250 boxes then I could ensure delivery by the first of the month.'

When we come to negotiation we see that the key element is to establish the other person's need and don't give anything away that costs you little if it's very important to them, but is less important for you.

Now let's role-play the widgets scenario again. You close the sale and your buyer asks, 'Could I take delivery by the first of the month?' but this time you *cannot* ensure delivery by the first of the month. What do you say?

I'm constantly amazed in seminars I run all over the world when I ask this question and people say, 'Tell him you'll do what you can.'

'I'll do what I can!'

Listen!

You can't deliver by the first of the month.

Fact.

If you say, 'I'll do what I can,' you are raising the buyer's expectations that you can deliver by the first of the month. In some cases a buyer will take that as meaning you are going to deliver by the first of the month. You have raised his expectation.

And you don't want to do that.

What you say is: 'Is taking delivery by the first of the month important to you?'

And, again, there are basically two options for the buyer. Option one is that it isn't important. So you needn't have gone into a blind panic and start thinking that you have lost the order! You can explain you can't deliver by the first of the month and discuss what is and isn't possible.

But what about option two, where it is really, really important to him to have delivery by the first of the month? Well, as Tom Hanks uttered the words apparently spoken by Jim Lovell on Apollo 13: 'Houston, we have a problem.' I don't deny that this is a major issue, but when would you prefer to start addressing the issue? Now, or round about the first of the month when the buyer's needs and expectations will have built up?

Just as the value of a service reduces over a period of time (more of that later), so the degree of disappointment, anger and frustration builds if the buyer is expecting one thing and you are expecting something else and at the end of it all the buyer feels he's been duped.

Buyers want honesty first and foremost, remember?

Don't you?

So it's better to establish the real need right now and begin to work out what is and isn't possible for delivery rather than deceive him. Partly because it's unethical and unacceptable and not very nice; but also because my brief to you was that it was important to build the relationship.

So the answer in all the four possibilities in this scenario is to find out the degree of importance; to find the real, emotional need. Don't guess, don't assume and don't just close the sale and miss the opportunity.

In other words, find out more about his need. Mobile phone operators took an age to realize the real potential of text messaging. Run by adults, they just didn't see young people's needs for quick, cheap and easy communication. If they'd done their research they would have been promoting texting years before they did when they found out the real market.

So the 'N' in the NAIL is for 'Needs'.

Time for the A in the NAIL and Chapter 8.

Ask and Accept the Answers

I had an engagement in Corby, Northamptonshire, with a pharmaceutical company. I was due to start at 9.15 a.m. at the client's offices just outside Corby and I was staying at the Hunting Lodge Hotel in Cottingham, just a few miles away. It's a nice Hunting Lodge. But they don't sell cuff links.

Now, when I am on a speaking engagement, I wear cuff links. NLP practitioners call it a 'positive anchor'. I call it getting in the right frame of mind.

And at eight o'clock that morning I realized I had no cuff links. I went straight down to reception and asked the receptionist if they had any. The answer was 'No.' The best place to buy a pair of cuff links was Corby. Now, it's not got a lot to say for itself, Corby. But surely I would be able to buy a pair of cuff links easily enough.

I first went to the client's offices and dropped off all my equipment and notes for the day, and was on Corby's doorstep at 9 o'clock sharp waiting for it to open. The first and most obvious place to buy cuff links was the local department store but they only had one pair. Big purple things with an image of Elvis Presley.

Not ideal.

The next menswear shop was for the under 25s and there wasn't a cuff link to be seen. So, at seven minutes past nine and aware that I was due to start the session in eight minutes' time, I arrived in what might best be described as a 'gentleman's outfitters'.

Perfect.

You can imagine my body language and my rushed tone of voice when I virtually ran in and saw several pairs of cuff links that were ideal.

'Can I help you?' the attendant said.

'Yes, I need a pair of cuff links. These here are fine,' I said, pointing to a simple pair of silver cuff links with no price marked.

For me, it was obvious what my need was. What would you do? Sell them to me and help me put them on? Surely, that would be the reasonable and sensible thing to do.

Do you know what he did?

He said, 'I have more round the back.' And turned to get more to show me! He wanted to impress me with his range, and I wanted a pair of cuff-links-to-go and to get out of the shop as quickly as possible.

I said, 'No, no; these are fine. I'll just take these ones.' And he said, 'Would you like them gift wrapped?'

Gift wrapped!

I am not making this up!

I'm manifestly obviously in a hurry and he wants to gift wrap them! In the event, his young assistant helped me on with them and I handed over the £10. I'd have gladly paid more because at the time I had a greater need than most people when buying cuff links. As I was leaving I heard the older man say to his young assistant, 'Ttttt! Customers …'

The point is that he couldn't accept my need because he didn't recognize it. He didn't even accept the answer to my question.

If you want to be truly persuasive you have to ask questions and accept the answers. You have to empathize with the other person and see the situation from their point of view. The cuff links salesman wanted to sell them and present them the way he wanted to, and not in a way that was appropriate for me at that time.

We are all guilty of telling people what we want to tell them and not what they want to know. We are all guilty of falling into a formulaic or prescriptive way of selling and persuading regardless of how the other person is feeling.

Stop it!

A IS FOR ASK AND ACCEPT

Start establishing the other person's needs by asking questions and accepting the answers. Stop telling people what you want to tell them and start telling them what they want to know.

'Turn features into benefits.'

Horrocks.

If you see the benefits of your offer as being xyz, it's unlikely your persuadee sees the benefits being xyz. It's more likely to be apxzd. In that order.

In Chapter 6 we talked about the importance of making it easy for people to buy. And the development of that important attribute of the good persuader is to ask good questions and not want to 'show off' about what you know.

If you want a role model for asking great questions, you could do worse than study Lieutenant Colombo in the old television detective series. Suspects spoke more freely because he lowered their guard. I wouldn't suggest you dress like Colombo or look foolish in front of your buyer, but I do suggest you ask questions in a disarming way to uncover his or her real needs.

I needed a skip recently. Not the sort you do with a rope but one of those big metal bucket things they leave on your drive and all your neighbours help you to fill up with rubbish before they come back and take it away. So I looked up 'Skip Hire' in the *Yellow Pages* and made the call to my local skip hire merchant.

'I'd like a skip please.'

'You'll want to know the price then?'

'Er, yes.' (Price was the last thing on my mind, but this is where I was being led.)

'They're £55 + VAT, £75 + VAT, £95 or £135.'

'Plus VAT for the £95 or £135?'

'No, they include VAT. They're builders' skips.'

'How big is each skip?' I asked. Price means nothing; she's telling me what she wants to tell me, not what I want to know.

'They're minis at £55, midis at £75, 6 cubic yards at £95 and the 8 yard builders' skip is the one at £135.'

Now if, like me, you are still wondering at this stage what you need, you are forgiven. I asked if she could explain to me how long and wide the four different skips were.

'What are you putting in the skip?'

At last, she thinks about establishing my need.

'Well, we are having our drive widened and we have rubble and stone to have taken away.'

'Oh, why didn't you say? You need the stone and rubble skips. The midi holds 4 ton and the mini about 3 ton. They're £75 and £55.'

I am not making this up!

What does four ton of bricks look like? I have no idea. Do I need a mini or a midi? Does the £75 and £55 include VAT? I have no idea. (There is no VAT on rubble skips but there is on 'furniture' skips but they include the VAT on the higher priced 'furniture' skips.)

Are you following this or have you lost the will to live?

I rather imagine this lady is still doing the very same thing now. Just telling her potential customers what she wants to tell them and not want they want to know in a manner they can understand.

For most people, cubic yards and tonnage, or mini, midi and 'builders' skips', is unknown information. And for us to understand it, we need to connect unknown information with known information.

Let me change direction for a moment and explain how people can learn through connecting known information with unknown information.

Unknown and known information – how people learn

My youngest son was doing his homework one night and I went upstairs to see if I could help. 'What is it you're doing, Seb?'

He said, 'I'm looking for the lowest common denominator.'

'Have they not found that yet? They were looking for that when I was your age.' Which I thought was really funny but he didn't think it was funny at all.

Then he turned to me and said, 'Actually, Dad, there is something you can help me with. In Geography tomorrow I have to explain the relationship between the earth, the moon and the sun. I've got ten minutes to talk to the class about how it all works and how big they are in relation to each other and how far apart they are.'

He had all the information, which I would like to share with you now.

The distance from the earth to the sun is 93,000,000 miles and the earth is 239,000 miles from the moon. The earth's circumference is 25,000 miles and its diameter is 8000 miles. The sun's diameter is 865,000 miles and the moon's diameter is 2140 miles.

Finally, the moon travels around the earth at a speed of 10 miles per second, the sun moves through space with a speed of 150 miles per second and the earth travels at 18 miles per second as it goes round the sun.

Eighteen miles a second! And you step outside today and there's hardly a breath of wind. How does that work?!

Now, if you'd drifted off into your own subconscious thoughts when I was on about skip hire, you're certainly forgiven if you have wandered off now. The information doesn't mean anything does it? What does 239,000 miles mean? You have no idea. You need to connect it with something you *do* know. So, for example, if you flew from England to New Zealand you would be up in the sky for around 24 hours and the plane travels at approximately 500 m.p.h.. So to go to the moon on a 747 would take about three weeks. That begins to put it into perspective. You are beginning to connect unknown information (239,000 miles) with known information. You can imagine what it might be like to be stuck in a plane for three weeks. That's an awful lot of movies and warm Chardonnay.

But Seb happened to have a football in his room and I took his ruler and measured it. As luck would have it the football was 8 inches across.

And the earth's diameter is 8,000 miles. We had ourselves a scale.

Now, on that scale of 1,000 miles = 1 inch, you can imagine the earth as a known size – a football. On the same scale the moon is about the size of a tennis ball (2.14 inches) and is just over 6 yards away (239 inches).

Imagine a regular size football pitch. In your mind's eye, see a football on the goal line and a tennis ball just outside the six-yard box.

The sun (93,000 inches) is one and half miles away. It's in a car park one and a half miles from the football ground and is 24 yards high. It's huge! And it's just one of the reasons why it's so hard to park on matchdays.

Let me give you another example. Imagine that the time from Christ's birth to the year 2000 was one day. Imagine that you were asleep as the clock strikes midnight as Christ is born. The Roman Empire disintegrates before you wake up and the battle of Hastings is just after noon. The 'Black Death' in Edward III's time reduces the population of Britain to a little over three million people at tea time and Henry VIII is on the throne around 6 p.m. The interesting thing about this particular connecting of unknown to known information is that the internal combustion engine doesn't get invented until the last hour of the day. I bought my first mobile phone at 10 to 12; the laptop, satellite navigation systems and so many of the things that we now take for granted weren't invented until just a few minutes before midnight. Indeed, Bill Gates became the wealthiest man the world has ever known in the 15 minutes to midnight.

Does this make sense now? We've connected unknown information with known information. It's how and why analogies work. It's how jokes work. It's often how people are trained. Effective lecturers and trainers use this technique. Take, for example, the often-used analogy of linking rocks and stones in a bucket to our time on earth. I'd like to meet the person (or at least know who it was) who first came up with this idea of this particular link. If you're not familiar with it, this is how it goes.

The lecturer is talking about time management. On his desk is a bag of sand, a bag of pebbles, some big rocks and bucket. He asks for a volunteer to put all three grades of stone into the bucket, and a keen student duly steps up to carry out the task, starting with the sand, then the pebbles, then the rocks, which do not all fit in the bucket.

'This is an analogy of poor time management,' says the lecturer. 'If you'd have put the rocks in first, then the pebbles, then the sand, all three would have fitted. This is much like time management, in that by completing your biggest tasks first, you leave room to complete your medium tasks, then your smaller ones. By completing your smallest tasks first you spend so much time on them you leave yourself unable to complete either medium or large tasks satisfactorily. Let me show you.'

And the lecturer re-fills the bucket, big rocks first, then pebbles, then sand, shaking the bucket between each so that everything fits. 'But sir,' says one student, slouched at the back of the theatre, 'you've forgotten one thing.' At which point the student approaches the bucket, produces a can of lager, opens it and pours it into the bucket. 'No matter how busy you are,' quips the student with a smile, 'there's always time for a quick beer.'

Right, where were we? Oh yes, you need to ask questions and accept the answers, but if you are to be understood you need to be able to reply in a way that is understood. Only the other day I had to buy 5,000 envelopes and there was a choice of two different envelopes at different prices. The salesman told me about the different weights of paper and the quality of the glues to seal and so on. But it was information I couldn't compare – certainly not over the phone. What I needed to know was whether the premium was justified. 'Imagine the cheaper envelope as a standard Renault Clio and the more expensive envelope as a top-of-range 5 series BMW.'

Now I understood.

Connect unknown information with known information. It's why I use so many analogies and stories in this book.

So that you can 'get it.' So you can relate the situations in menswear shops, car showrooms, stationers and so on to your own situations.

So the A in the NAIL is for Ask questions and Accept the Answers.

The flaw in the NAIL

As with all brush stroke acronyms, there are flaws. The flaws in the NAIL lie in 'ask and accept'. The first flaw is that sometimes people lie. So how do you spot it and what do you do about it? The giveaway in lying is in the body language. If the body language is not consistent with what's being said you need to test the answers that you're given again. And you do that by asking supplementary questions. Such as, 'Can you tell me more about that?'

And the other flaw in 'ask and accept' is that sometimes you know more about a client's requirements than they do. Occasionally a buyer is given a brief by someone, but *they* don't know the full detail; so again, it's important to test the answers by using such questions as, 'Would it be useful to look at an additional xyz if you're looking at abc?' This way you can tease out of the buyer their lack of knowledge. What I really mean by 'ask and accept' is that you must accept the buyer's attitudes, beliefs, views and thoughts. You don't necessarily accept they're always telling the truth, nor that they know what they're doing.

Time for Chapter 9.

Implications and Influence

When I worked in advertising we did some work for the local football club, Leeds United. Bill Fotherby was the managing director well before Peter Ridsdale set to with his 'ego and egg' strategy, which is basically the ego of the chairman egged on by his cohorts, but with little real grasp of economics and no 'Plan B'.

Bill asked me to look at the sale of season tickets and how we might increase the number sold. Now, buying a Premiership season ticket is for the committed fan. You are paying in advance for 19 games of football. You are paying in July or August for a product you will still be 'consuming' the following May.

And whilst I don't know of many products that people are willing to queue up for in the rain as football fans do for Cup games (indeed I don't know of any other product where people will be so blindly loyal for a lifetime regardless of how the product performs), it is clearly a big commitment to make for someone to pay in advance for a variable product.

And what of the people who were supporters and wanted to see some of the games, but didn't want to go to all of them? So we came up with the idea of buying a third of a season ticket. We would split the 19 games into three 'lots' of 6, 6 and 7 games. We would 'grade' the attractiveness of the teams so that each 'lot' was roughly equally attractive and sell a ticket for a third of the season for a third of the price. Less cost and less commitment but allowing the fan to ensure he or she would see some games and feel like a real supporter. And once they were committed, hopefully we could go on to sell them two thirds of a ticket and build them up to being a full season ticket holder.

Brilliant.

So Bill liked this idea and suggested we go and see Mavis in the ticket office. Mavis had been working in the ticket office for some years. It was she who saw the queues for the big games. It was she who sold the tickets over the counter to season ticket holders and regular 'match-by-match' buyers alike.

So my colleague Richard and I went to see Mavis and I proudly explained the idea. She listened intently and then looked at us with some contempt.

'You don't understand, do you?'

I looked at her with a look that said, 'What?'

'The people who queue up here,' she said, glancing at the ticket office window, 'don't think further than next week. You come here with your fancy Filofaxes and your time management ideas and your schedules and you think everybody lives that way. Well, they don't. They live hand to mouth. They don't plan. They don't schedule stuff in their diaries weeks ahead. They queue up at the window.'

So off, with our tails between our legs, went Richard and I.

I'd asked Bill questions and accepted the answers. Now I'd asked Mavis questions and had to accept her answers. I hadn't worked out the *implications* for the other person. And that's what Chapter 9 is about. The *implications* for the other person.

Or people.

I IS FOR IMPLICATIONS AND INFLUENCE

My wife and third son, Sebastian, share a car. I say share a car, but at the time 'her' car was due to be replaced Seb had just started learning to drive. Isn't it great being 17 years old and you're learning to drive? Do you remember that first real taste of freedom?

Anyway, Madam had decreed that her Rover 25 was to be replaced and off we went one morning in January to look at various cars. Now, neither of us is passionate about cars. In fact, we are not really interested at all. Different strokes for different folks. I could spend all day looking at guitars (and have done – lovely days); and The Goddess could spend all day looking for a dress (and has done – not great days); but cars? Frankly, I would be happy if we bought a car and were back home in time for morning coffee.

(I do like the smell of a new car, though – don't you? What a great emotional trigger. To the best of my knowledge no one has been able to bottle it and produce aerosols of the stuff. It's as emotive as baking bread when buying a house, garlic and tomato as the ferry pulls into Napoli and cigarettes and cheap burgers when you go to a big football match.)

Back to the story.

At the first dealership, my wife sat in the driver's seat of a small hatchback and did what pretty much everyone seems to do when sitting in a new car. She kind of looked around. What are you doing when you are looking around? You have no idea, have you? You don't know what you are looking for (or at). You are just deciding whether emotionally there is a 'fit'.

As she was doing so the salesman with his big coat came over, leaned into the car via the passenger side open window and asked, 'What do you think?'

My wife pointed to the dashboard and declared, 'It's got no wood.'

He looked at her quizzically, and whilst I had guessed she was referring to the little bit of oak veneer in her Rover 25, he was none the wiser.

'I'm sorry?' he said.

'It's got no wood here.' Pointing to the dashboard. 'Mine's got some wood there.'

'Well,' he replied with ever such a slight smirk, 'we can always put you a bit of wood in.'

She smiled the smile of a woman who was not to be patronized and we left the dealership. He hadn't created any empathy, he hadn't established her need and he hadn't 'got it'. That this was one car buyer who wasn't interested in the same aspect of cars that he was interested in.

And so it was by coffee time that we arrived at the local VW dealership. And what a delight and education that turned out to be. We were greeted by a young saleswoman of about 23 years old. She asked what we were looking for and we explained that we were looking for a hatchback. She, in turn, explained there was effectively a choice of two – the Golf and the Polo. The car will probably do less than 5,000 miles a year and was not a major investment so we said we would like to look at the Polo. Perhaps out of mischief, or perhaps just because my wife was really into the oak veneer on her Rover, she sat in the driver's seat and said to the salesperson, 'It's got no wood. Mine's got a bit of wood here.'

'You mean the oak veneer on the Rover? Yes, I like that too,' said Lorna. But VW don't do oak veneer. All the empathy in the world, but accepting that you can't always do something about objections. Isn't that true? Sometimes you just have to come clean and explain that your service doesn't have that feature.

So the conversation went on and she, quite rightly, asked my wife what she was looking for, and if the Polo was fitting the bill.

And then she did a really neat thing. She asked *me* what I was interested in.

'Safety,' I replied. 'I quite like my wife and I certainly like my 17-year-old and I'm interested in how safe this car is. I won't drive it,' I continued, 'but if I had my way I would have a man with a red flag walking in front of this car to ensure they would have a safe journey.'

'It's the only car under £10,000 with side air bags,' Lorna said.

Get in!

She had worked out the implications for me in this sale. She had established *my* need. She hadn't talked about brake horsepower or how quickly it goes from 0 to 60. Is that turning features into benefits? Well, it is for someone who is interested in that, but it's not for me. That's why just turning features into benefits is horrocks.

So we said we would think about it (how to deal with that objection in Chapter 11) and we went home to discuss things with Seb.

'Can I get involved in this decision, Dad?' It was, after all, to be 'his' car. And I could see more material for my book looming, so of course he can get involved!

We returned to see Lorna the very next day. A buying signal if ever there was one.

Now, before we did so it was important to look at other cars. It was important for him to *want* another car if we were to get the best deal on the Polo. When we come to look at negotiation, if yours is the only show in town you can hold your price better than when there is a little competition. More of that later.

'Hello,' said Lorna. 'This must be your son?' gesturing to Seb. 'Hello, Mr Hesketh,' she said as she shook the 17-year-old learner driver's hand. He visibly flexed his shoulders and brought himself to his full height. The thing is, you don't get called 'Mr Hesketh' when you're 17, do you? Well, obviously if your name isn't Hesketh you don't, but you know what I mean. It was lovely for him and made him feel important.

She asked *him* what he would like to look at. He recalled the conversation we had had, and could he now look at the Polo?

And he did that funny thing of sitting in the driver's seat and looking at the dashboard, and he didn't know what he was doing either!

Again, she did the neatest thing. She asked him what he was interested in.

'Has it got alloy wheels?'

She looked at me and I looked at her and we both went to look whether or not it had got alloy wheels.

'No it doesn't, but ...' (guess what?) 'they are available at extra cost.'

Get in!

And then she got even better. She asked again what he was interested in. 'Does it have a CD player?'

'No it doesn't, but ...' (guess what?) 'it is available at extra cost.'

Get in!

She had established his needs. She had asked questions and *accepted* the answers.

We were nearly there.

My wife, my son and I had different needs and different priorities. And the implications of the purchase were different for each of us, too. The implications for me were that my wife and son were happy and safe. The implications for my wife were that the car was economical, easy to run, easy to service and so on. And the implications for my son were what his friends would think.

And that's a big implication when you're 17.

In the business-to-business selling situation, how often are you selling to a group of people? Almost always.

Do they have different needs? Yes.

Are there different implications for these people after the sale? Yes.

Can they all buy? No.

Can they all influence, and will they all have a need to feel they have influenced so that, in turn, they think they have been involved? Yes.

And so it was with Seb. Does he have any money? No.

Can he influence? Yes – big style.

I believe that what went on in his head he himself didn't actually think through, and fully understand. I believe that he felt the decision was pretty much made by his mother and I. But he wanted to play his part. He certainly had power of veto and if the thought of owning a Polo filled him with dread I wouldn't have gone ahead. But he wanted to influence. The implications for him of *not* influencing the decision a little (by choosing the alloy wheels and the CD player) would be that he wouldn't feel he owned the car. He wouldn't feel as proud. He wouldn't enjoy it as much. He might even feel a little resentment.

He wanted to be involved.

And so it is in business. There are people in the buying circle who have the power to write the cheque but don't feel the need to influence. Enlightened managers allow their people to make decisions. They understand the importance of their people feeling they are involved. When people own a decision they are much more likely to a) make it work and b) enjoy their job more.

There are also people who have huge influence but have little or no buying power. The point is, you have to *plot* the people you are trying to persuade in the business-to-business (B2B) situation. Ability to buy on the vertical scale and ability to influence on the horizontal. And you not only have to establish each of their needs by asking questions of each of them, but also establish the implications for each of them in buying your service, product, idea or excuse.

What are the ramifications for the IT guy if this goes wrong?

What are the ramifications for the FD if the terms aren't right?

What are the ramifications for the whole deal if you exclude the MD's PA?

And so on. You need to know the implications for the other person.

I worked on the Wallace Arnold account for a little while. They are coach tour operators who sell coach holidays to the 'older end'. My dad was into his 70s and wouldn't go on a coach holiday because, 'They're for old people, Phil.'

The creative team at the agency wanted to show their prowess by having a lovely shot of the Scottish Highlands (nothing wrong with that); but a large coupon for people to respond ruined the 'look' of the ad.

And the creatives weren't for turning despite the client, Gordon Durrans, consistently telling us that the coupon needed to be bigger.

Because the older your target market is, the more likely it is that the respondents will have trouble with their eyesight, have arthritic hands and therefore trouble with writing in small spaces. It was only when I invited a group of people in their late 70s into the agency to look at the creative work, and the creative people could see the difficulties the septuagenarians had with filling in the coupon that we managed to get bigger coupons in the ad.

And response increased.

It was about the implications for the other person.

Often, in what's sometimes known as 'Big Ticket Selling', the top management is most interested in the return on investment. They want knowledge and they want improvement and that means money. You've got to talk figures when you're taking to the big cheese.

The department heads are usually interested in a solution to a problem. On occasion, a solution to ease his or her life. Sometimes they don't really want the best price (but may have to be seen to be getting and asking for the best price) and the operators are interested in 'downtime' and ease of working. And so on.

I've always wanted a Mont Blanc pen. The big fat one.

It's an emotional thing – as all purchases are. But I couldn't bring myself to buy one and spend what is, quite frankly, an obscene amount of money for a fountain pen. At the time they were £250.

For a pen!

But a time came when my wife said she would like to buy me the Mont Blanc for Christmas. We went to a store in Harrogate called Jespers, that has a fine range of Mont Blancs, Watermans, Cross, Parker and other quality brands.

As we entered the store the managing director, Peter Jesper, by chance was serving.

'Can I help you?'

'Yes,' I said. 'I'd like to look at that pen there.' Pointing to the mother and father of all pens that I had not ever handled in my 40+ years.

'Would you like to try it?' I nodded and he carefully laid out a little velvet cloth (NB: always treat your product with the utmost care and attention) and slowly opened a bottle of Mont Blanc ink.

I was enjoying this and so was he.

I handled the pen and unscrewed the top. I dipped the pen into the ink and began to scribble on a piece of paper he had also lovingly prepared for me.

And as I wrote with the Mont Blanc pen for the very first time, it was like writing with an old-fashioned quill pen. It didn't glide – it juddered. It didn't feel like silk, it felt like sandpaper.

Oh no!

All these years I've wanted one and it's rubbish!

'Would you like to try the Waterman?' asked Peter Jesper. Now, I was here for the ride. This was the antithesis of the need for cuff links so, yes, I would try the Waterman. And this time it *was* like silk. It was like putting on an old friendly jacket.

But I didn't want the Waterman.

So what would you do now, dear reader? In my seminars I ask this question and I almost always get remedies. I get solutions. Particularly from men. Problem? Solution. Sorted.

Wrong.

Peter Jesper said a great thing that I suggest you say if you know someone likes the brand you are selling. 'What do you like about the Mont Blanc?'

'I don't know,' I replied with blunt honesty. 'I've always wanted one – I just like the Mont Blanc – the big fat one.'

'What are you thinking of using it for?' Peter asked.

'I've no idea.'

And I hadn't. I just wanted one. Like most people, I sign letters and cheques, fill in forms and write little notes to the milkman (nothing soppy; just a request for an extra pint now and again, that sort of thing).

Now, one of the key issues for persuasion as we work through this book is to establish the other person's need. But not necessarily the other person's need in terms of what they will do with a product or how they will use a service, but also in terms of how big their *emotional* need is. In the last chapter we looked at the scenario of establishing how important it was to have delivery of 200 boxes of widgets by the first of the month. In this scenario we are exploring the importance of how high an emotional need there is. When we come to look at negotiation this is absolutely critical.

Back to Jespers.

Then Peter Jesper said another really neat thing. 'Many of our clients use the Mont Blanc as what they call their "contract pen". You look like the sort of gentleman who might sign big contracts.'

Get in!

Not only did he call me a 'client' (I like that); but he thinks I'm the sort of 'gentleman' who signs big contracts. Pre-nuptials and the like.

He's making me feel important.

And that, in persuasion, is really important.

Make your persuadee feel important. Don't patronize and don't be insincere. Don't be dishonest and cynical. But make the other person feel important. By listening with rapt attention; by focusing on what they are saying because, right now, they are the only person you are interested in. And you are really interested. If you're bored, you're boring.

De facto.

He said, 'A lot of our clients find the Mont Blanc scratches a little at first.'

'That's what happened to me,' I said. He knew that, of course, and continued, 'Can I suggest we try other nibs and that you hold the pen in a slightly different way?'

Only *now* does he start to find solutions. He has found my need and established that the Waterman, good as it is, is not the pen I've come for.

'It comes in an attractive black leather holder sir; if you wish you could look at the three pen holder so you could complete the set with a roller ball and a pencil at some stage.'

And that's what I did. Because he established my need – my emotional need – before he started offering solutions.

In this scenario there is little in the way of objections. So often, it's the objections that are the stumbling block and we need to address them. I'll come back to that in Chapter 11.

So the 'N' in the NAIL is for Need(s); the 'A' is for Ask questions and Accept the Answers; and the 'I' in the NAIL is for Implications, which give you a much better chance of Influencing when you have fully uncovered and explored them with your persuadee.

Time for Chapter 10 and the L in the NAIL.

CHAPTER 10

Thinking Long Term, Acceptance Time and Closing

Let me tell you about a Ralph McTell song. It's on one of the 17 albums I have of his. The song, 'Sweet Mystery', is about a young man wanting to do the 'right thing' in courting a young girl instead of finishing up in the mess in which he always seems to find himself. It goes like this:

> One of these days I'm going to do it right,
> Take her out to dine by candlelight,
> Rent a suit and give my shoes a shine,
> Talk about nothing over a glass or two of expensive wine.
> One of these days I'm going to do it right,
> Get to her door and just say goodnight,
> Even if she asks me to come in,
> I'll make myself say 'no' so I can call again.

Because he's thinking Long Term. And the L in the NAIL persuasion process stands for Long Term.

L IS FOR LONG TERM

I was at a client conference recently, and after my talk the sales director got up to speak; and at the end of *his* brief talk said to his sales team, 'And don't forget the ABC – Always Be Closing.'

Horrocks.

ABC – Always Be Selling perhaps, but don't always be closing. That's what old-fashioned salesmen do and it won't do now. It can ruin the sale.

Of course, if you take thinking long term the wrong way, you could end up not closing. And you don't want to do that.

When do you close?

When you know how much the nail hurts and the dog (remember him?) knows what you can do about it.

If you *do* want a formula or process to follow, this is it. This is selling in the NAIL process.

1   Find out the need – how much does it hurt?
2   How deep is the emotional need and can you amplify the need? Ask questions and accept the answers.
3   What are the implications?
4   What are the ramifications for the buyer buying today or not buying today? Can you build the pain of the nail and help the buyer picture himself away from the nail? Discovering the requirement is not necessarily an opportunity to sell. You need to know the implications.
5   Influence the buyer.
6   Only talk benefits that are relevant to the buyer. Only talk about matching his needs with your offer.
7   Test close.
8   Think long term but always act short term. Ask if certain conditions are met whether they are in a position to buy. But don't ask a direct question unless you are sure you will get a 'yes', as it's not so easy to regain the ground once you have had a rejection. Test closes are expressions and questions such as: 'How do you feel about that?'; 'How does that strike you?'; 'Are you happy with everything we've discussed so far?'
9   Ask for the order.
10 Shut up.

How are *you* perceived throughout this process? Many years ago people in advertising talked about the 'USP' – the Unique Selling Proposition. And, at the time, brands often had a unique 'thing' to offer. But in today's business environment it is very, very difficult for the majority of companies to have a truly unique proposition for longer than a Bank Holiday weekend before their competitors have copied their very 'uniqueness'.

So, often it's *you* that is the USP. It is you that has the Unique Selling *Persona*. It is you who makes the difference. Remember, people buy people first. Most of my clients sell products and services that you can't buy unless you have a relationship. Again, going back to the world of advertising, the frequency and number of times a typical consumer gets to see a TV commercial is measured by the 'OTS' or 'Opportunities to See'. In persuading in a long-term relationship with a client or potential client we need to talk about Opportunities to Interact (OTIs).

Opportunities to Interact

Think of the relationships you have with your friends. Apart from some very special relationships you have – deep relationships forged either over time or under times of great stress, great enjoyment or a lot of time together – relationships wither on the vine if you don't keep seeing people. Over the years we have met some fine people on holidays. Friends for a week or two who, if they lived nearby, would undoubtedly become very close friends. The sort of people who would come to our children's weddings. But the distance means that we don't see each other and, as a result, eventually they even drop off the Christmas card list.

So it is with business relationships. You need to find opportunities to interact with your clients. Keep in touch; go and see them but for goodness' sake have something to say when you do. Because if *you* don't see your clients your competitors certainly will.

And you don't want that.

Back to closing and step 8.

Closing should be as simple and easy as, 'Will you marry me?'

In my seminars I ask if anyone has asked this question and the other person said 'no'; or if someone has asked the question of them and they have replied in the negative. Rarely does anyone say it's the case. On the handful of occasions it has happened there's a great story! One guy, Jeremy, put his hand up at a seminar I was running. 'You've asked someone if they would marry you and they said "no"?'

'Four times.'

'Four times?'

'Four times,' he confirmed. 'Four different girls.'

'How well did you know the girls?' I asked.

'Well, perhaps that was the problem; I didn't know them at all well!'

So, he made my point for me. You don't typically ask someone to marry you until you are both sure. Now, it would be easy to say that the business environment is different; that in the business world there are greater time pressures; that people have to do business with people they wouldn't necessarily socialize with.

But that would be missing the point.

The *principle* is still the same. Find out the needs, the emotional needs, work on the gap between you and them and pop the question when you're confident you will get an affirmative answer because you have already asked the test question. Look for your persuadee saying things such as: 'We're thinking of ...' 'We're exploring the possibility of ...' and keep saying, 'How would that affect you? Why is that important?'

Now back to step 9. When at the end it's all gone quiet.

The theory (which I accede to) goes that if you are selling and persuading, and you have closed and asked for commitment, the next person to speak 'loses'. Now I'm not sure about the word 'lose', but I do agree that shutting up and staying well and truly shut up is the best thing to do. After all, you have nothing else to say and all you want is the client to agree. So give the client time to think and give him the next chance to speak.

No matter how long it takes.

Sometimes people need 'acceptance time'. Ever had a parking ticket? Frustrating, isn't it? And not easy to simply shrug it off. In a year's time you won't remember paying it but at the time it's annoying. You need 'acceptance time' whilst you come to terms with it. When sportsmen and women have achieved an unlikely result they are often asked how they feel about their victory by journalists. 'It hasn't sunk in yet,' they often reply. When people experience great personal tragedy it often takes time to digest the enormity of the change they are experiencing.

Over the course of one season I recorded all the interviews with the winners of the major knockout football competitions in England. The results were clear and revealing. The most often used expression by professional footballers after they have won a trophy is 'Unbelievable', closely followed by 'Absolutely unbelievable'. Not known for their wide vocabulary, professional footballers. And when asked for the key to their success the most popular response is 'Belief' closely followed by something along the lines of 'Great set of lads'. So they think it's unbelievable but the key reason they have won is their self-belief. Excuse me? Crazy? Not really; just acceptance time and, of course, a limited vocabulary, which doesn't help.

Often it takes years to accept change.

In this book we don't deal with the process of how people react to great trauma, nor to great personal victory and achievement. But interestingly, the 'process' that people go through is bizarrely similar.

There are reasonably clear and systematic changes in self-esteem during a tough or dramatic transition. Often it starts with what might best be described as a feeling of numbness, followed by a denial or unbelievability that this wonderful (or tragic) thing or event could have happened to them. Then it starts to 'sink in'. With particularly bad news it can lead to depression before there is an acceptance. For those who have had good news, this then starts them off on a new 'plan'. They have won the League or the Cup but now the planning starts for next year. For really bad news there is a need to search for meaning and internalizing before testing acceptance and working on how to move on.

We need to accept that people need acceptance time. Later in this chapter we look at the importance of understanding this process; not from the persuader's point of view (you're off onto something else or banking the cheque or delivering the widgets), but from the persuadee's point of view. They are now stuck with the widgets and how you handle that persuasively has a huge bearing on your next interaction with the client.

Back to silence.

So shut up. But what happens when you shut up and they do too?

Forever!

It happened to me when I was selling to a client the notion of paying a fee for some work we would do to test his ads. I'd worked on the 'Power of One'; that in order to reduce the size of the 'gap' between me and him, Pat Chambers of Suite Ideas, I reduced the apparent size of his investment.

Pat and I had agreed in principle that he would pay us a fee to produce ads that he could test against his own ads to see if we could improve the quantity and quality of his response.

'So how much, Phil?' asked Pat.

'Well, you spend £700,000 on advertising, Pat. If you were to spend just 1% of that budget on the test it would only require you to improve the effectiveness by just over 1% to justify the investment. Would you agree?

'So I propose we work on a fixed budget of just £7,000 for this work and for that we will produce artwork for you to send direct to the publications. We could do all that and have ads ready for the key Easter period if you gave your go-ahead today. Can I assume we can go ahead?'

And I shut up.

Pat, being a good salesman himself and knowing all the techniques, did too.

He smiled.

So did I.

Who would end this deadlock?

Importantly I had nothing else to say, so stayed silent.

He was partly experiencing acceptance time and partly testing me out, as so often the persuader is put off by silence and starts jabbering about reducing the price.

So if it ever happens to you, say this: 'I read in this book recently that when the buyer is silent it means he wants to go ahead – was he right?'

And the most important thing is to shut up again!

Use it; it works.

Do you recall the story of my wife and I looking at the house we currently live in, and her saying with her eyes, 'Say nothing

– we're buying this house. This is ours.' That was only the start of the story.

My wife hasn't been on my course. Indeed, she's never seen me speak. I can't get a word in edgeways at home.

But she used the 'Power of One' that night.

We drove home in silence. The house was everything we could have wished it to be apart from one thing. It was more than we could afford. Well, perhaps one other snag. It needed gutting. There was no plumbing to speak of, the bathrooms and kitchens were as they had been built in 1925 and there was dry rot under the floors. Oh, and it needed a new roof.

And to cap it all, we had three children under 5.

'We simply can't afford it,' I said. I accepted that it was the house of our dreams, but at £90,000 (*that wasn't the actual price but I've used a figure of £90,000 to allow me to illustrate the point*) and no possibility of the vendor negotiating, it was not possible. I had done all the calculations and even allowed for us selling our own house quickly and at its top price. I had assumed we would live in a caravan on the drive for as long as needed, working in advertising by day and re-building the house by night, but I couldn't see a way, at that precise moment, of how we could come up with £90,000.

'Well, what *can* we afford?' she asked. I looked at the calculator again. I punched in all the numbers assuming I would make no pension contributions, maximizing on the loan I could get with my current salary and assuming full value for the house we were sitting in. '£86,500.'

'Pass me the calculator,' she said and held out her hand. She continued, 'If we were to live in that house, how long would we live there?'

'Well, it's a couple of steps up the property ladder for us. And it's very near the school the boys would go to and the youngest is four months old. If he went to the school and went straight through sixth form then we would still be living in the house in 18 years' time. 18 years minimum, I'd say.'

And then she paused and her expression changed as she looked at the calculator, and with her head down she said, 'So the difference is just £3,500.' She tapped on the calculator. 'That's just £194 a year.' She tapped four more times. 'That's just £3.74 per week.'

There was no sound then from my wife apart from this quiet, but impassioned, plea: 'So it's come to this has it? I'm living with a man who for £3.74 a week will stop me having the house of my dreams? £3.74 a week.'

We still live in that house. The Power of One.

How did we do it? We found a way ...

The final – but key – aspect of thinking long term is all about buyer's regret or what I learned in studying psychology as 'cognitive dissonance'. To understand cognitive dissonance better, it's worthwhile defining the meaning of the two words.

A 'cognition' is a belief – and we have all got them, remember? Festinger described *cognitions* back in 1957 as 'the things a person knows about himself, about his behaviour and about his surroundings.'

'Dissonance' is the feeling resulting from two *non-fitting* or *contradictory* beliefs or bits of knowledge about the world. In other words, if an individual simultaneously holds two cognitions which are psychologically inconsistent it's an unpleasant feeling, so the subconscious mind sets to work to reduce the dissonance either by adding some 'harmonious' cognitions, or by changing one or both cognitions to make them 'fit' better or be more consistent.

For example, if individuals smoke but also believe that smoking is bad for their health, they experience cognitive dissonance; so need to stop smoking or work on the belief that we're not here long and they would rather die than get old. Cognitive dissonance is typically experienced by people making a major investment, such as a new car. They spend the money and know that as they drive away the vehicle has already depreciated in value. They are experiencing cognitive dissonance or 'buyer's regret'. If you have felt it, it's okay – it's normal. This particular 'buyer's regret' explains why car brochures are typically read by people who have just bought the car rather than people who are *thinking* of buying the car.

So as persuaders, what can we do about it? Earlier in this chapter we touched on how there are reasonably clear and systematic changes in self-esteem during a tough or dramatic transition. If you are in the business of selling, you will no doubt have experienced the feeling of achievement when your buyer has bought. They have committed themselves to your widgets (or whatever) and you feel pretty pleased with yourself. You have been on a roller-coaster of emotions, hoping the buyer will commit to your company and finally you have reached the top of the loop. The drive home feels like it's all downhill. But where is our buyer on this roller-coaster?

They are now stuck with your widgets and are typically experiencing cognitive dissonance, or buyer's regret (see Figure 10.1). Will they sell them on? Have they paid too much? Have they done the right thing? So whilst it's a great sale you have made it's also a great time to help develop the relationship further and differentiate yourself from your competitors. And this is not just about selling widgets, is it? In professional services I consistently get feedback from buyers, that 'the big guns' with the sharp, expensive suits and empathetic smiles come in to pitch for the business and are never seen again.

It took me a long time to really appreciate this one as I sold a service too. I couldn't afford (and the company couldn't afford) for me to get involved in actually handling a client's account, so I foolishly – for many years – stayed away once the business was won. It was only in my 40s that I fully realized the error of my ways. The client doesn't

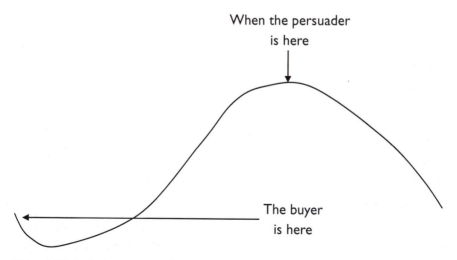

When the persuader
is here

The buyer
is here

Figure 10.1 *Roller-coaster of emotions*

expect you to be at their beck and call. They don't expect to see you at their offices on a weekly or monthly basis. But they do want to know that you *care*. They do want you to make that unsolicited phone call to ask how things are. On more occasions than I care to itemize, a phone call to the MD at the client end to check on progress unearthed a 'situation' that could easily be put right. In the past, clients had simply felt unloved and uncared for and voted with their feet.

So, in summary, particularly if you are persuading someone to make a substantial investment, remember buyer's regret. Remember that they are most likely to experience cognitive dissonance (they are not in control of their subconscious – remember?) and keep in touch.

It can be as simple as offering them a free sample of something that will be launched soon and you would value their opinion on it. Better still, call them a week or two after the purchase and ask them how they *feel*. Just knowing you care can make a huge difference to them using you again, recommending you, and you yourself feeling like what you are doing is worthwhile. And we all want that, don't we?

Why do hotels treat you better when you arrive than when you leave? Arguably it's more important to treat you well and help you with your bags when you are going, because it helps the memory of the stay and encourages you to come back and recommend. Delegates at conferences are always telling me stories of how they got more sales and recommends by calling back on satisfied (and dissatisfied) customers and clients. Both First Direct and Vodafone are excellent at calling me from time to time to check it's me using my credit cards or mobile phone if I'm out of the country for a while. They build up empathy, trust, credibility and, of course, loyalty. And we all want *that* as well don't we?

Let's move on to objections and negotiation.

PART 3

Overcoming Objections and Negotiation

CHAPTER II

Objections, Negotiation and Making More Money

A book on persuasion and influence could not be complete without addressing the issue of the 'cold call'. Telephoning an unknown prospect to sell an idea, product, service or indeed, just make an appointment, is one of the toughest things to do.

I know. I've done it and have several T-shirts to show for it. It can be an extremely costly and deflating business, and if it can be avoided by judicious use of mailings, advertising, leaflet drops and other marketing means then these routes should be pursued. If you are looking for a recommendation on overcoming the reluctance to pick up the phone to make that call, here is my advice.

Create a 'pain gap' of time and give yourself an incentive at the end of it. Personally I typically allocate one and a half hours that is scheduled in my day in advance. During those 90 minutes I don't take calls, I don't take interruptions, I don't drink coffee and I don't gaze out of the window or check my e-mails. I plan my calls but, importantly, I don't start with the easy ones first. I put myself in a mindset of going to the dentist's and do nothing else but cold calls for the 90 minutes. At the end I reward myself with a coffee and a biscuit and, if necessary, extend the time frame if I'm not achieving as much as I set out to do with my cold calls.

When I was working with new salespeople I would have us all sit in a room together. Typically there would be four of us and I would effectively 'lock' us all in the room. With four phones there is literally nothing else to do. That factor, coupled with hearing others calling and having a degree of success, had a marvellous effect on the others.

I would go so far as to tell *other* colleagues exactly what we were doing so that we were really committing ourselves to doing it.

It worked. Create your own 'pain gap' and go for it.

OBJECTION MANAGEMENT

Let's get on to handling objections, then. What are the first three things you should do with any objection?

1   *Let the other party clearly state their objection in full.* The more heated they are, the more you need to listen with rapt attention until they have finished. The more agitated they are, the more they will not hear anything you say in reply until they have said what they need to say.
2   *Agree with the person objecting.* Empathize and let them know that you can see it from their point of view. And remember, avoid using the word 'but'. They see it as an objection, so you need to create empathy first by appreciating the validity of their objection. You have to see it from their point of view just to get on the dance floor.
3   *Ask if there's more.* Make sure you get the whole thing out.

Let's take a simple objection first. Suppose you want someone's time to discuss an issue and they say, 'I'm far too busy.' The key is to repeat what the other person says. So your response should be, 'I can see that you are very busy.' They will often go on to explain more: 'You've come at a bad time. I've got all this work to do, a deadline I can't shift and there's no way I can see you now.' Again, reflect it back: 'I can see this is not a good time for you and you've got a lot on.' And remember to let them know you understand how they must *feel* about it. You are making emotional investments in the other person. Most people don't do this, so if you display genuine empathy it makes you different. You are building up the obligation to them seeing you (more of that later). Importantly, you're also building trust. Often the other person then asks you what you want and sees you as an ally – someone who appreciates his or her issues and how hard he or she is working.

Do it. But be absolutely sincere.

I was running a seminar recently when a delegate asked me: 'Can you teach me how to fake sincerity?' I thought he was joking but it turned out he was asking me in all sincerity. Or as much as he could manage, anyway. I suggested he get another job.

As far as making a sale goes, I believe that objections are great opportunities rather than barriers. But how do you turn an objection into an opportunity?

Let's look at it step by step.

Step 1: Prevent the objections from arising in the first place

For example, if you know that your product or service is more expensive than your competitor's, address it early in the meeting. You can't run away from it because the prospect is bound to find out eventually. Then concentrate on the positives, like *why* you are more expensive. Why is it better? How is it stronger? What can you do that the competition can't? And *most importantly,* what are the *intangible, emotional* benefits that you can offer over and above your competition? 'Peace of mind' is a superb example of an intangible benefit. Make sure you have some impressive answers already worked out before you start persuading.

Indeed, if you know that the prospect has a major objection and it's not easily resolved you have to *dissolve* it. If you keep presenting knowing the 'bomb' is going to go off at some point your prospect isn't listening anyway. His subconscious is focused on the problem. So raise it very early on. For example, distance between you and your prospective client might be a big issue:

Salesman: 'I'd like to think that our service is relevant but we are 200 miles from your head office. Do you see that as an issue?'

Buyer: 'Yes, I do.'

Salesman: 'Should we address the issue now?'

The buyer is bound to answer in the affirmative – in fact he will be pleased that you have brought it up. Once he's agreed the 'issue' (not a 'problem', remember) needs to be 'aired' importantly, you ask *him* to start. If you break the issue down into several smaller issues, you can often dissolve it by showing that the ramifications are not as bad as he thought.

Step 2: When you know what the objection is, the next thing to do is *agree with the persuadee*

You're not agreeing that they are right, but agreeing that there is an issue that needs to be addressed. Phrases like 'I can understand that', 'I'm glad that you raised this point' or 'Some of our best customers thought that at first' will avoid conflict and reduce the importance of the objection in the prospect's mind.

Step 3: Discover the *real* objection

Often people raise price as an objection when really it's something more fundamental that's stopping them moving forward with you. The first and most important thing to do is to get to the heart of the objection. To do this, ask some searching questions. If it's a price objection, find out just what the problem is. Is it outside the company budget? Is it more than they can authorize? More than they expected? Dearer than the competition? Questions such as 'Compared with what?', 'What would that mean to you?', 'Why is this important to you?' or 'How much did you have in mind?' can start to get to the heart of the objection.

But at the same time, don't assume everything is an objection. I was in Harrods recently and asked the salesman what kind of person spent £6500 on a pen. Instead of telling me (and flattering me that it was people like me) he simply went on to show me Mont Blancs at the very bottom of the range. Why assume it's an objection?

If the objection is that they need a response very quickly, explore the need by saying things like: 'We *could* get back that quickly, but it won't be very good'; or 'We couldn't possibly do it the justice it deserves without spending some time exploring the answers to these questions'. I always use this tack and, on more occasions than not, more time is often made available if it means the difference between a good, measured response and a knee-jerk reaction. I would say, 'There is a quick and easy, ready-made solution to every problem.' And then pause before adding, 'Unfortunately it's usually wrong.'

Often you get more time because the first objection turns out not to be the main one, once the client has thought through the implications of getting a quick response. And anyway, you never talk to 'the Big Cheese' until you know your maths. The 'Main Man' wants numbers.

Often it's politics that create objections. People like to haggle for control of money, resources, decisions; and, of course, other people. In short, they like to score one over their rival in the company. Getting to the heart of that little topic is not just a completely new subject – it's a whole new book by itself.

Step 4: What is the *expectation*?

A friend of mine, Mike Baxandall, invited my wife and I to his wedding 'fest' a few years ago. He and Liz had known each other for many years and both were entering their second marriage. We were delighted to be invited, but had no real idea of what a wedding 'fest' was. All we knew was that the evening affair was to be in a marquee in the grounds of their house and that there was to be a jazz band. So the nature of the venue, the invitation itself, and Mike and Liz's light-hearted attitude to the whole wedding 'thing' led us to believe it was to be a reasonably low-key affair. They had actually married the week before with just immediate family present. So, in our *perception*, this was a summer barbecue type of event. As we were preparing to go my wife commented that she would probably not know many people and that she would drive.

It turned out to be the best night out of the year! We knew a lot of people there, the jazz band were sensational, the marquee, the food, the ambience, the gospel singers, the wine – indeed, everything, was first class. And one of the key elements in enjoying ourselves so much (we abandoned the car and got a taxi home in the wee, small hours) was that we were not *expecting* it to be that special. You see silver medallists unhappy with their gong because they came to win whilst bronze medallists are delighted – because their expectation was just to get to the final. Newly-promoted teams to the FA Premiership are happy with fourth from bottom, whilst fourth from top is a disaster for a top club. It's all about expectation.

EXPECTATION AND THE 'PYGMALION FACTOR'

Pygmalion was an interesting guy.

In Greek legend, the story goes that a brash young sculptor in Cyprus – called Pygmalion – thought that all the women on the island were terribly flawed in one way or another. So he took it upon himself to carve a statue of his ideal woman, embodying every feminine grace and virtue. For months on end he toiled away with all his apparently prodigious skill until he had fashioned the most exquisite figure ever conceived by art. The story goes that he did such a good job that Pygmalion fell passionately in love with the statue, and could be seen in his studio kissing its marble lips, fingering its marble hands and generally dressing and grooming the figure as if he was looking after a doll. However, in spite of the work's undoubted loveliness, Pygmalion was desperately unhappy, for the lifeless statue could not respond to his warmth and love. He had set out to shape his perfect woman, but had succeeded only in creating frustration and despair for himself. It would be a pretty sad end if the tale ends there, but it doesn't. According to the scribe who wrote all this down, the goddess Venus took pity on Pygmalion and brought his statue to life, and – da daa – he and 'Galatea' (as he named her) blushed, embraced and married with the goddess's blessing. All lived happily ever after.

A load of old horrocks? Maybe, but after an excellent study by Rosenthal and Jacobson in 1968, the 'Pygmalion Factor' became part of the lexicon. Basically, two American academics, Robert Rosenthal and Lenore Jacobson, had become increasingly concerned that teachers' expectations of lower class and minority children were contributing to the high rates of failure among these types of students. It's what my English teacher wife calls 'teacher expectation'.

So they carried out an experiment in a state school in a predominantly lower class, but not impoverished, community. At the beginning of the school year, the researchers gave the students an intelligence test they called 'The Harvard Test of Inflected Acquisition' to give it a bit of gravitas.

They told the teachers that this test could determine IQs and also identify those students who would make rapid, above-average intellectual progress in the coming year, whether or not they were currently 'good' students.

Before the next school year began, teachers received the names of those students who, on the basis of the test, could be expected to perform well. Unbeknown to the teachers, Rosenthal and Jacobson had actually picked the names from the class list at random so any differences between these children and the rest of the class existed only in the heads of the teachers. The 'Inflected Acquisition' test from Harvard was of no value.

When the second intelligence test was administered at the end of the year those students who had been identified as 'academic spurters' (sorry, this is American research) showed, on average, an increase of more than 12 points on their IQ scores, compared with an increase of 8 points among the rest of the students. The differences were even larger in the early grades, with almost half of first and second grade 'spurters' showing an IQ increase of 20 points or more.

Teachers' subjective assessments, such as reading grades, showed similar differences. The teachers also indicated that these 'special' students were better behaved, were more intellectually curious, had greater chances for future success, and were friendlier than their 'non-special' counterparts.

In essence, a self-fulfilling prophecy was at work. The teachers had *unconsciously* encouraged the performance they *expected* to see. Not only did they spend more time with these students, they were also more enthusiastic about teaching them and unintentionally showed more warmth to them than to the other students.

As a result, the special students felt more capable and intelligent. And they performed accordingly.

It wouldn't be allowed now, would it? Fact is, this is going on all the time. Your people will achieve more if you expect them to achieve more. Your own children are more likely to achieve more and do more if you gently expect more and tell them there are no limits to what they can achieve.

> I am sitting at home in the aftermath of the English football team losing to the French by two goals to one in Euro 2004. Interestingly, England were not really *expected* to win the game before kick-off. But as the match entered injury time, England were winning 1–0. So expectation had been rising throughout the second half that England not only could, but would, gain a famous victory. When France scored a goal in the second minute of injury time English supporters were desperately disappointed – they were so near a win. When France scored a second goal with the very last kick of the game to win the match, the whole of England was devastated. The players were at least a day getting over it. Because expectation had risen.

So it is for you. Don't raise the buyer's expectation more than you need to. And certainly don't allow it to rise inadvertently by letting your buyer *assume* that you can deliver on Friday or have it in a choice of colours if you're unlikely to be able to fulfil your promise. When new starters joined our company I used to give them one piece of advice on day one. I would say, 'Just do what you say you are going to do and you have a career here. If you don't remember anything else from your first day in this company take this away. Do what you say you are going to do.'

So in entering the field of 'objections' we are effectively talking about expectation and negotiation. Managing expectation, understanding negotiation, knowing when the other party is using 'tricks' and when they are just looking for a reasonable resolution. Let's look at the key issues for negotiation and this whole 'win-win' thing.

UNDERSTANDING NEGOTIATION

Negotiation is going for a walk. Negotiation starts the moment you begin the persuasion process. Negotiation isn't a stage that you get to; it's not a milepost or a hurdle, it's built into the whole process. If you take that on board you begin to see the importance of building your own value, the persuadee's perception of you and your value proposition right from the start. Clean shoes, being on time and all that. Negotiation *is* the journey, so enjoy the journey but, most importantly, make sure you're always walking. Negotiation is about people. Just as companies don't appoint ad agencies, companies don't negotiate with companies. In the most part, people meet people.

Arguably, negotiation starts when the persuader and the persuadee are conditionally committed to the 'sale'; and negotiation generally results in a compromise between persuader and the persuadee. Typically, the seller reduces something (often what he charges) and the buyer increases his offer from his starting position. But that's only part of the story.

The relationship is critical – *relationship negotiating* is the ideal if you want to get the most out of the 'deal'.

So the much touted 'win-win'?

I think that's horrocks.

Well, sometimes at least. Allow me to explain. A lot of buyers want win-lose, don't they? They don't care about your position so long as they win. It might well be short-sighted, immoral, unethical and unfair, but the buyer is paid to get the best price. The lowest price he can. And in many circumstances in today's environment (thankfully not everyone) he or she doesn't care if you go to the wall.

Do you remember the film *Pretty Woman*? In the movie, Edward (Richard Gere) picks up a hooker, Vivian (Julia Roberts). He's from the East Coast but in LA for the week. He has picked her up by accident and agreed a fee for an hour. But as far he is concerned she is far too preoccupied by time. He wants to relax and chat.

'How much for the entire night, Vivian?'

'To stay here? You couldn't afford it.'

'Try me.'

'$300.'

'Done.'

He has certainly raised her expectation of how much she can charge by agreeing quickly (more of that later). In the morning, as Vivian enjoys a relaxing soak in the suite's magnificent bathtub, he has what he describes as 'a business proposition' for her. 'Vivian, I'm going to be in town until Sunday; I will pay you to be at my beck and call 24 hours a day for the rest of the week.'

She thinks about it and says, 'If you're talking 24 hours a day it's going to cost you,' and works out that $300 x 2 x 6 is just under $4000.

Vivian: '$4000.'

Edward: '$2000.'

Vivian: '$3000.'

Edward: 'Done.'

At this point, arguably we have a 'win-win'. She has got more than he offered to pay and Gere is paying less than she first asked. A reasonable compromise. But then she can't help herself. She thinks that even $3,000 is an obscene amount of money. She's delighted.

As he turns to leave for work she blurts out triumphantly, 'I would have stayed for $2000.'

'I'd have paid $4000,' he replies.

What's that? Lose-lose!

In the *relationship,* no one's happy. Because what matters is what the other person *thinks* they have got. It's their perception of the negotiation that matters. It's managing their expectation. It's allowing them to think they have a got a good 'deal' in the broadest sense of the word 'deal'.

So what matters is not whether *you* 'won' or *they* 'won' but, rather, whether the 'deal' you have struck is acceptable to *you* – regardless of whether or not the other person *thinks* that the deal is acceptable to *them*. And, remember, this isn't just about money. Let's use the word 'OK' to describe an acceptable deal.

Companies are forever charging different prices for the same thing. So in theory anyone who hasn't got the best price has 'lost'. But that doesn't take into account all the other factors such as time of booking, need, knowledge etc. etc.

So let's not always just think, 'win-win'. That's naïve. Instead, let's focus on ensuring you have got a deal that you are happy with in the circumstances and, most importantly, you have allowed the other party to *think* they have got a deal that is OK for them. That is, think either, 'I know I've "won" and you *think* you've done OK', or 'I'm OK and you *think* you've done OK.'

Bit more wordy than win-win, I agree, but more realistic. The key is that the other person needs to *believe* they have done well.

Imagine you have seen a house with your significant other. Suppose you have a budget of £800,000 and as you are viewing the house you think it's perfect. Everything on your 'wish list' is here in this house. It's the right location, near to the amenities that you need, it has the right number of bedrooms, bathrooms; the garden is just the right size and so on. And the more you look around the more you are looking at each other and saying (without speaking!) that it's a bargain. It's everything you want it be and you just don't see why they are asking only £800,000. You have been looking at houses in the area for some weeks and this is the one for you. You are emotionally involved and you want to buy. You feel like bursting into song. What do you do?

Well, not bursting into song is a good start.

Do you tell them it's perfect? Do you let them know you think it's a bargain? Do you rush in with an offer at the asking price?

No.

Why not?

Because you already know that the key is to let the other person *think* they're 'winning'. And this, if you know what you're doing and can control all the urges of your subconscious (which is controlling you 95% of the time, remember), is what you do.

1   Don't let your body do what it wants to do.
2   Don't give away how keen you are or they will think they can get more than £800,000.
3   Create empathy.
4   People *sell* to people they like just as people *buy* from people they like. But you don't want to add value to the house, so compliment them on the internal décor. In effect, tell them what you like about it without saying you think the house is priced too low.
5   Don't agree quickly.
6   If you rush in with the full price they aren't going to think they've 'won', are they?
7   Let them think it's a struggle.
8   Let them know you can just match their price but give the distinct impression that £800,000 is absolutely at the top end of the range. Maybe put an offer in? Better still, ask them what they would be

prepared to accept. Because you don't know their position. They might be even more desperate to sell than you are to buy. Putting to one side the issue of surveying the property and so on, does this make sense?

The point is, it's not about 'win-win'. Arguably you would be willing to pay more than £800,000 so in effect they've lost. But what if they would be delighted to take £750,000 for a quick sale because of their circumstances? Now you've 'lost'. It's about finding out the other person's perspective.

Let's talk about neat negotiation. Time our seventh acronym. This is NEAT – NEAT negotiation. Here's the first NEAT.

N is for Never put a marker down first

There are a number of interesting things that emanate from the negotiation in *Pretty Woman*. Vivian didn't fully understand that $1000 either way didn't make as much difference to Edward as it did to her. She put down a remarkably high 'marker' for *her* but it still didn't faze *him*. He was willing to pay the $4000 but negotiated just for fun.

Once she asked for $4000, that was the most he was going to pay. It never crossed her mind that he would pay more. And once Edward offered $2000, that became effectively the minimum *he* would pay. She would have gladly settled for $1000!

When I worked in advertising I used to run a number of interesting events for clients and potential clients. I did that because all the research (qualitative, quantitative and anecdotal) said that clients hired and fired advertising agencies for two key reasons – creativity and relationships. If the agency was creative (in the broadest sense of the word) and if it had a good relationship with the key people, the client stayed on board. Put either or both of those things in jeopardy and the client started to look around. So I wrote what I hoped were creative communications and invited clients to 'creative' events in order to meet them and form relationships.

We went land yachting and water painting, did fly fishing and archery, and also held a number of seminars on body language, goal setting and so on. I was in conversation with John Foster at Dunlop

Slazenger one day when he mentioned he knew a golf psychologist. Now this interested me. Other people did golf days and one of my criteria for organizing an event was that I wasn't willing to do something someone else did. But the idea of getting together a dozen or so clients and potential clients with a golf psychologist held an immediate appeal.

So I got the golf psychologist's details and called him. He had impressive credentials and worked with some big names. I asked him what would be involved in a 'Golf Psychology Day' if I provided 12 players, the golf course and paid the course fees, the meals and so on.

He explained that he would arrive at 8 a.m. and suggested the clients arrive at 8.30 a.m. for breakfast. Over breakfast he would talk for about 30 minutes on the psychology of golf. After that we would go on to the putting green, each with a putter and a ball and he would explain the psychology of putting. Following coffee we would go onto the practice ground and, starting with the lofted clubs and working up to the longer irons, we would practise chipping on to the practice green whilst he told us what we should be thinking about.

After a break for lunch we would stand on the tee for a full 20 minutes whilst he would share with us the ideal thoughts for standing on the tee. And then we would play a round of golf whilst he accompanied different groups talking to us about our mental state. And, believe me, we would be in a mental state by this time.

At this point in the conversation I'm like one of Pavlov's dogs. It sounded perfect. The clients I had in mind (indeed, the clients who came along) would between them spend over £50m on advertising. And most of it wasn't with us, I can tell you.

So I asked him the price. How much do you think he will charge for the day? I'm picking up the bill for the golf course, the food and the drinks. Everything apart from him.

So how much would you charge? What's reasonable? I was thinking he might be in the range of two to three thousand pounds, but I didn't know. He might well be out of my price range and over £5000 a day. I ask this question at my seminars and almost always have one or two who are expecting the price to be in excess of £10,000. I'm willing to pay over £1000 but if it gets over £3000 I'll have to think hard.

'So how much do you charge for the day?'

'£400.'

£400! Like me at the time, you may now be experiencing two knee-jerk reactions. Firstly, marvellous! It's well within my budget and is only £30 a head. The green fees are more than that – in fact, so is the catering for the day. It's a bargain.

But there's another thought going on inside my subconscious and I'm certainly not in control of the fear gripping me at this point. Is he any good?! Can he possibly be the best in the business if he charges only £400 a day?

Two key issues here. Firstly, he put his marker down first so what's the most I'm going to pay? £400. Secondly, perception of value and price are inextricably linked. So, if you can avoid it, don't put your marker down first. What is important to them?

Whether you are buying or selling, find out the other person's need. Do you remember the discussion on buying 200 boxes of widgets in Chapter 7? Explore their need if you can before you put your marker down. And, if there is flexibility and you have to put your 'offer' in first, go as high as you possibly can if you're selling and ridiculously low if you're buying. Find out what the other person needs, including personal and emotional aspects.

And remember, some people cheat! I have often had a client say, 'Well, wxy has already offered me £z' when no such offer has been made. If you suspect the client is cheating you need to explore and test whether it's a true offer by asking for more detail. More of that later. I've also known clients to 'plant' a letter on their desk that appears to be a bid from someone else so I get a false impression of the competition.

And, in case, you're wondering about the value of the golf psychologist; yes, he was good. Worth £400 of any corporate budget, I'd say.

E is for Empathy

People buy from people they like and sell to people they like. So listen intently; see it from their point of view but separate the people from the issue.

Why is the relationship so important? Because unless your product offer is itself unique, you're the only part of the deal that is. *You* can create a unique position for your product or service, as we said in Chapter 10, by becoming the *Unique Selling Persona*. That's about building trust, rapport and empathy with the other person. And whilst establishing an impression of uniqueness is a very effective technique when you are selling, denying 'uniqueness' is a really neat ploy when you're buying.

Let him think he's 'won'. The key benefit of *not* putting your marker down first, or going for your highest or lowest plausible offer, is that it is more likely to mean that when you move he thinks he's done well.

The Mexicans have a saying that 'every cock crows on his own dunghill'. Buyers, in particular, tend to like the power that their ability to buy gives them. Some abuse it, which is a shame, and some are intoxicated by it. Which is a tragedy for them when they leave the job and find their friends were just suppliers. Indeed, to throw another quote in within four sentences, Henry Kissinger paraphrased Lord Acton who, in turn, paraphrased the British Prime Minister of 1770, William Pitt, by saying 'Power corrupts. Absolute power corrupts absolutely.'

Accept your persuadee will enjoy being powerful and let him or her have their power. Accept his or her power but then move into your area of expertise.

Perhaps even buy the other party a small present. Well before the real negotiation starts. It builds empathy and obligation. Lastly, a great thing to say when you are unhappy with someone's price offer and you want to retain empathy is, 'I think I might need your help here ...' instead of 'Can you reduce the price?'

A is for Ask about their interests

Of course, the ideal situation is to know exactly what your buyer (or seller) wants before you talk figures. Often your persuadee's personal and political needs are important too. The bigger the deal, the more significant these factors become.

Sales people tend to forget that when you sell to someone in a large organization, the buyer is staking his reputation on you, so you need to understand all of his needs and concerns by asking questions. Ask him or her how they *feel* about the situation. Ask what the implications are and what will happen after the transaction. Ask what the downside might be of using a competitor. Ask about their interests. Only then can you begin to understand what the implications, costs and perceived values are.

And if you really want to buy that £800,000 house, why not have a friend put in a bid to see whether the vendor will negotiate with *them*?

If necessary, ask the other negotiants – away from their office – what is important to them. A café, a restaurant, a golf course will often elicit a different (and real) answer compared with the one you might get when they're sitting on their own dunghill.

When I worked in advertising, we won the Spam account. What a marvellous advertising account to win it was too. The PR value was completely out of proportion to the advertising spend, but we loved it and benefited from it. I was interviewed on BBC Radio 5 and quoted in the *Sunday Times* and the *Wall Street Journal*. Happy days. One of the best things about handling the Spam account was going to their golf day run by Newforge Foods. Spam for breakfast, Spam for lunch, Spam for dinner, Spam golf balls, Spam umbrellas and Spam tees.

I am not making this up. The only thing missing was the cast of *Monty Python* performing their Spam sketch. Of course, this was before the days of the Internet, when Spam wasn't an expression for unsolicited e-mail, but rather filled you with nostalgia – not to mention pressed meat.

Anyway, the marketing manager, Rob Lucas, had asked us and five other agencies to pitch for the account. We had an 80% chance of failure until I spent an evening on board the *Canberra* during a marketing conference and found out the real needs and desires of Rob and his colleagues. Once I had asked all these questions away from the office, listened with rapt attention and knew the bigger picture, we were probably in with an 80% chance of success.

Ask about their interests and find out what's important to them.

T is for Think: 'The other party need to *think* they've done well'
So some of the time win-win is horrocks, but it's important for you to know at what point you will walk away; to know what is the *least* you will settle for. If you know the point at which you will settle, it's an

important stage in the walk. Look for aspects of your offer that are of low cost to you and high benefit to them, and don't give these away lightly.

I only book on conferences at short notice. I sell days pretty much like airlines sell seats and once the plane has taken off and the date has gone you can't have it back. So I don't commit myself to attend a seminar or talk as a delegate until a day or two before. One such seminar I like to attend is the Institute of Sales and Marketing Management annual conference in Birmingham. The day before one annual conference I was in Berkshire, and at 3 p.m. called to see if I could have a ticket for the next day. There had been a cancellation, so all I now needed was a hotel in Birmingham. Now, I'm not as familiar with Birmingham as I might be but when this particular conference is on, the central hotels are fully booked.

So eventually I called a hotel on the outskirts and they had a room. 'My name's Hesketh – I will be there around 7 p.m..' I hadn't discussed price, so that when I got there it might be an interesting negotiation.

Imagine the scene. It's a little after seven o'clock in the evening in October. It's dark, cold, wet and windy. I run into the hotel from the car park with laptop over one shoulder, overnight bag over the other and briefcase in hand. I look a little like a wet waif. The 'acknowledgement' from the male desk clerk barely registered as one at all. It was a slight lift of the head and a furrow of the brow.

Positive first impression? I don't think so.

I gave him my name and the first time he speaks is to give me the price. 'It's £75, bed and breakfast.' I thought I'd try the intake of breath and the 'best price' techniques first (more of those in a moment). Now what would your reaction be as the hotel receptionist? Look at the implications for me of going somewhere else. All he needs to do is to make me *feel* good and make me *think* I've done well. Something along the lines of, 'I appreciate it's a cost sir, but most hotels are much more expensive in this area and we are anticipating being fully booked.' He could even go on to fix for a porter for me. Make me *feel* I've done OK.

But no.

He looked at the screen, he looked at me wet, bedraggled and ready for a warm bath and a cold beer and said, 'I could do it for £65.'

Wazzock!

Then I said, 'Is that your best price?'

And he tossed his head from side to side, puffed and blowed, and said in a questioning sort of a way, '£55?'

He is literally giving money away *and* he's not making me feel like I've done OK. His body language is suggesting to me that there's more to be had! I've effectively got a free dinner and he's lost margin because he didn't understand the persuasion process. He didn't understand my *need*, he didn't *ask* me any questions, he didn't see the *implications* of me going somewhere else and he didn't make me *feel* like I had 'won'.

Yet it could have been so different, so easily. Most of all this was done through body language and grunts.

Summary? As we discussed with Edward and Vivian, remember the other party needs to *think* they have done well. Let's further explore this question of, 'Is that your best price?' The value in this book for you personally – not just the money you paid for it but the time you have invested in reading it – is in the next few paragraphs. I absolutely guarantee you will save money and make money both in your personal and business life if you use this question regularly *and* at the right time.

The Goddess and I are in a furniture store. It is only two days before we go on a four-week holiday and it has been decided that we are definitely buying a new three-piece suite today. It is the time of the summer sales and bargains are to be had. We are definitely buying today – from this very shop. Indeed, we are definitely buying the three-piece suite we are sitting on. The 'marked' price is over £6,000 but today the price is a little under £4,500. We are giving the sales lady all the buying signals. Not only empathy but also sizes, formats, colours and textures are pretty much agreed. We go to the sales lady's workstation and she inputs onto the computer. With the protective coating and delivery the total cost is £4,678.

Would we like to go ahead with a 10% deposit?

At this point the sales lady (particularly if she is on any sort of commission) is feeling that this particular fish is hooked and is being reeled in. And it's at this point – when the sales person is calculating the commission in their subconscious (they're not in control of that, remember) – that you change your body language.

I pull back in the chair. I grimace. I am having second thoughts and say so to my wife. I say to her that it's a big investment and that perhaps we should go on holiday and think it over. The sales lady gives away her feelings by her expression. The fish is wriggling off the hook.

Then, and only then, as I make to stand up and walk away do I say these words I am asking you to say that will guarantee you will save money:

'Is that your best price?'

She says, 'Let me see what I can do ...'

Get in!

She taps away on the calculator as my wife stands impassively by. 'My absolute bottom price is £4,500, Mr. Hesketh. I know it's only a gesture but it's the best I can do.'

£178 is a gesture! I can buy a new guitar with that! Relative to £4,500 it might seem like a gesture but I've just saved myself £178 because we were happy to buy at £4,678.

I puff and blow (so she thinks she's done OK) and, with a few looks between my wife and I, we agree.

As she recalculates the deposit and tells us about delivery times I ask her for her calculator. Just for my own interest I time myself pulling back, grimacing and saying 'Is that your best price?' It takes 15 seconds and I make £178. I tap the numbers into the calculator. At this rate I am earning over £42,000 an hour.

Result!

Now here's the second NEAT.

N is for Neutralize your body

Or to put it another way, 'Don't let your body do what it wants to do.' If you really, really want 'it', don't let the other side know. Never give the impression of wanting anything too badly.

Which brings me to the 'Intake of Breath Syndrome'. You're doubtless familiar with it. The seller gives his price and the buyer has a sudden intake of breath or grimaces. It could be a painful bout of wind but the chances are he's going for the simple and low key approach of, 'That's more than we had in mind.' Alternatively, he may opt for the more extravagant approach typified by a sharper, more audible intake of breath followed by a theatrical puffing of the cheeks and an exasperated exhalation.

How often is this genuine and how often is it a ploy? Well, who knows? What I *do* know is that if you use the intake of breath *regardless of what you think of the price* you will save money – a lot of money – over the course of a lifetime. Remember our golf psychologist? I have trained myself when buying always to use the intake of breath. Despite my surprise that he wanted just £400 I still used the intake of breath. Do you know what he did? He said, 'Well, I won't charge you travel expenses if you think it's too expensive.' It was a tempting offer but I would still be racked with guilt if I hadn't paid his bus fare. He was a good guy and a nice guy and deserved to be rewarded accordingly.

So if you think the price you are being offered is a bargain, don't act like a Springer spaniel and wag your metaphorical tail. Brace yourself to act like it's too much or don't react at all. If you are selling and you believe you are asking for a premium, don't allow your perception of price to affect the buyer's view. One of the key issues for retailers I work with who sell a premium product is with their own salespeople in the stores not believing anyone is willing to pay such a premium. When you are being paid less than £10 an hour it's hard to accept that someone is willing to pay £100 for a pair of shoes, £250 for a pen, or £5000 for a work of art. But you have to see it from the other person's point of view and not react.

Don't let your body do what it wants to do. You are not in control. Remember, 95% of your thoughts and actions are controlled by the subconscious, so unless you tell your horse what to do, the other person's horse will work out your reaction and neither of you knows what you're doing.

As a persuadee you can read the degree of interest in the other party by how they move. A chin stroke is a positive sign and someone pushing forward whilst their hands are under their seat is another. Remember that the closer people are, or want to be, the closer their patterns of behaviour. If you are persuading, mirror the body language; if you are buying or feeling uncomfortable don't let your body do what it wants to do.

But back to the intake of breath. What if someone uses the intake of breath on you? Well, he or she might think it's a 'big ask' – or maybe they've been on a course! Here are five things to do if someone uses the intake of breath syndrome on you.

1 Become more extreme. 'Hey, that's my price now – it'll be more in six months' time.'
2 Repeat the price. 'That's right!'
3 Intentionally misinterpret. 'I know – it's a great price, isn't it, when you think of xyz?'
4 Do nothing.
5 Use 'feel, felt, found'. It would be neat to attribute this to the original author but my research suggests it's lost in the ether. However, the principle has stood the test of time and I offer no apology for repeating it here if you haven't come across it before.

Many situations can be eased by 'feel, felt, found.' Imagine someone is shocked at the premium you are asking. They react and wait for a response. It's important to choose your own set of words but just as important to use 'feel', 'felt' and 'found' in that order. So, for example: 'I can understand how you feel. A lot of our satisfied customers felt just like that when they first saw the investment. But what they found was that the durability and the 24 hours service [etc.] made it worth every penny.' So insert your own response in each situation: 'I understand how you *feel*. Many people *felt* that way, but they *found* that …'

E is for Equate everything in the deal
Professional, well-trained buyers tend to break up and separate your offer and negotiate what appears to be the whole but then ask for other things once the price is agreed. They can erode your position piece by piece, so it's important to keep the whole package in mind at all time.

In the early 1990s Maastricht, a small town in the Netherlands, became forever famous, as it was there that members of the European Union went through some hard bargaining to ensure that monetary union was secured before the year 2000. Many were not keen to allow any member states to have exemptions. Where exemptions *were* allowed, the French argued that dates should be agreed when these countries would join the monetary union. There were also disputes over the future of the Social Chapter, which would allow for certain rights to be given to workers in the work place. The French said they would block the Treaty if these measures were not included. The British, on the other hand, were adamant that they should not be included, and would therefore block the Treaty if the measures were included. At the negotiating table, John Major said, 'Some colleagues won't sign without the Social Chapter; I won't sign with it'.

The result of the negotiations was that Britain was granted two major opt-outs; one from the Social Chapter and one from economic union. *The Times* said: 'Major wins all he asked for at Maastricht.' The *Daily Telegraph* led with: 'Out of the summit and into the light' and *The Economist* wrote: 'The deal Tory ministers and most backbenchers had been praying for.'

I recall John Major having what was almost a mantra during the negotiation of the Maastricht Treaty – 'Nothing's agreed until it's all agreed.'

Nothing's agreed until it's all agreed.

Don't give things away that have a value to your buyer (or seller) without recognition for it and don't agree until it's all agreed. Get the other person's full 'shopping list' before you start to negotiate

You are not a mind reader. And although the other person may not be totally open and may need some prompting, he or she may not even have thought through all the possible variables that are of interest. So keep exploring and looking for them. The more variables you find the less you will have to give on price, and the more added value you can build into the deal.

Keep accurate notes and show that you are doing so. At some point say, 'Does that include everything?' and draw a horizontal line across the page to suggest in the strongest terms there is nothing else to bring into the negotiation.

I've known buyers to conveniently forget things that I have thought were agreed, so taking notes is very important. Keeping notes shows that you are professional and allows you to summarize at any point.

Don't assume that everything in legal gobbledygook is not negotiable.

We all believe the written word.

Beware the devaluing of services over time and don't say, 'We can tie that up later.'

Don't agree, then look at little concessions afterwards.

A is for Agree only with a struggle

Let's go back to 'I'm OK– you *think* you've done OK'. The key issue is that the other person needs to feel or believe that they have got a good 'deal' in the broadest sense of the word. Clearly you know what is acceptable to you (and remember, it's important for you to know the point at which you will walk away from the situation if you can); and you need to let the other person think they have got a good deal. If they don't, they may wish to renegotiate then or later. If they're not happy they may take some other action that doesn't meet with your approval.

So only agree with a struggle. Lead them to believe that you have gone as far as you can go.

Do you recall in Chapter 9, when my youngest son and I went to the VW dealer and were interested in buying a Polo? I wanted to get the best price and it was important to find out the sales lady's lowest price. It was also important to give the impression that we could walk away. This is what happened.

On the drive to the VW dealer I said to Seb that he needed to be really keen on another car. 'But I'm happy with a Polo, dad. Why should I want to be keen on another car?'

'If you're the only show in town you charge the top price. If you don't have an alternative, how can you agree with a struggle?' So he decided that the Renault Clio was his choice. 'What do you like about the Clio? What colour do you prefer? What will your friends think of the Clio? What do you like about the drive?'

'Why do I need the detail, dad?'

'Because if Lorna's been on a course she will have been taught to 'test' the objection and she will ask you what you like about the Clio to see if it's a negotiation ploy or a genuine preference.'

'OK.'

So after we had been through the shenanigans of CD players and alloy wheels we sat down to talk numbers. Lorna made an offer for the Rover 25 and worked out the difference I needed to pay and I did the old 'intake of breath'. She asked me what sort of figure I had in mind, which already meant that she had to reduce her demand. I asked if that was her best price and suggested a particularly low figure, which meant that we were heading for stalemate.

And then, good as gold, Seb pipes up, 'Perhaps we should go back and look at the Clio, dad?'

Get in!

Lorna visibly recoiled. 'Oh. I thought you were keen on the Polo. What do you like about the Clio, Seb?'

And he told her, missing out the bit about it being a fabulous bargaining tool. At 17 you get to be interested in cars and he was able to talk detail. (If someone says something along the lines of 'I like your presentation and your offer but this is all I have in the budget', you have to test whether it's a genuine budget issue or a ploy. You test it by taking something out of your offer to bring the price down. If they are not interested in the cheaper alternative it's likely they can afford the full package.)

Eventually we agreed a compromise figure and she asked me what I did for a living. I had asked far too many questions during the two days. And I asked her if I had really got a good deal. 'Yes. You got such a good deal that the sales director said he hopes we don't lose money on it.'

I like that a lot. Now, I don't know if it's the truth but she gave me the impression that I had 'won' – that I had done 'OK'. She gave the impression (and so had I) that I had only agreed with a struggle. So if it's an important negotiation, crawl through the process towards the end – don't just walk.

And don't just 'split the difference' to achieve an 'I'm OK– you *think* you've done OK' result. Let's imagine you want £100,000 for a product and they offer £80,000. Let's also assume that you would be happy with £90,000. You would be satisfied to split the difference. Firstly, don't jump in with the suggestion. You are not agreeing with a struggle and as soon as you have gone to £90,000 there is little or no chance of you getting any more. Wait for them to suggest splitting the difference. Next, dwell on the fact they're willing to pay £90,000. Get a clean sheet of paper and write the two figures down. 'So you are suggesting £90,000 and I was asking for £100,000. We're not too far away now, are we?' *Then,* after an acceptable waiting period, suggest splitting the difference at £95,000.

Throughout the negotiation reduce the size of your 'giving-in', and don't let your last concession be a big one or they'll think there's more to be had. It's all about closing the gap and letting them believe they have got a good 'deal'.

Time for a final acronym (within an acronym) in this chapter.

CRAWL through the negotiation

C – create a climate for them to really value what you offer. For example, the phrase, 'What you are asking for is exactly what we specialize in. We are ideally suited to your needs' would create such a climate. And, don't forget, it's important to also create a climate for *them* to think they've done well in the negotiation.

R – raise the perceived value of what you do. Aim high if you're selling and justify the premium via intangible benefits. If you are a buyer, aim low so you reduce the *perceived* value of the service or product to you.

Think of your maximum (or minimum) plausible position and whatever you're doing, remember that your first stake in the sand sets the limit on your best possible outcome.

A – avoid deadlock – keep walking. There are, of course, times when you accept stalemate. However, if you have developed the relationship in the right way and both know that you would like to progress, then don't shut the door.

W – why *not* go for a high price if selling or a low price when buying? Firstly, you might get it, and secondly you are giving the impression that as you move your position, you are agreeing with a struggle.

L – leave room when you start (but not too much). We recently had a bathroom salesman come to the house, and after he had measured up gave us a quote of just over £20,000. I hadn't even had time to raise the eyebrows and begin the intake of breath before he said, 'But we have an offer on at the moment and I can do it for £10,000.' He certainly needed to leave room for negotiation but to drop so quickly by so much takes away all the credibility.

So let's summarize the key issues before we move on.

1   Use the intake of breath syndrome if you are buying and ignore it if you are selling. Or use one of the other four techniques.
2   If someone says what you offer is expensive, agree with him or her. Say, 'Yes it is. But look at what you get.' And then talk about the emotional, intangible benefits to that particular client.
3   Towards the end of the negotiation walk say, 'Is that your best price?'
4   When someone says 'I want to think about it', you say: 'I agree you should think about it. Often when our clients say that it's because there's a particular issue they need to address. Is that the case with you?'
5   Don't just 'Split the difference.'
6   Beware the 'forced time ploy'. Establish at the start of the meeting how much time the buyer has. If you are selling, don't tell your buyer you have a plane to catch. If you're buying you might want to consider it, but beware dishonesty and the ramifications for the long-term relationship.
7   Talk about what they *want* first (remember the NAIL).
8   I get people to tell me what they want – I establish how much they want it – then I tell them that's exactly what I do and talk price once they're walking up the path.
9   Sell value, not price.

10   Know what your bottom line is.

11   If you are selling, empathize and understand that it's the *beginning* of the process for the buyer and not the end, as it is for you.

You have been through the 'new toy stage' and had a learning curve. As you close the deal don't just get bored, walk away and think about your next 'conquest'.

12   The best thing a salesman can have is a hot referral. And the best way of getting a hot referral is to call your buyer after the sale and ask how things are. But be honest, sincere and genuine and truly care. Or don't bother.

A great thing to say after you have closed the sale is 'Thank you for your faith in me (us).' It shows the buyer that you appreciate it's a bit of a gamble for him or her and creates greater empathy.

T is for Tie up all the details

When persuading and you feel that the deal is done but you're walking on ice, it's very tempting to leave all the details to later. Perhaps you don't want to mention that mileage costs will be added on, or to remind them that VAT is payable, or that there's a delivery charge etc. But if your buyer isn't expecting additional costs it may make all the difference between using you again or not. The customer who pays the bill and doesn't come back often is the one who doesn't give you the feedback.

Beware the buyer who reluctantly pays but says nothing at all. And months down the line it's just too late to recover. All my service industry clients tell me similar stories. They win a client, they have a relationship, they take the relationship for granted and the client has started a new relationship and worked with someone else on a project before they find out. And they all tell me it's usually too late to recover the situation at that point. They didn't point out all the details at the time of buying and they created the direct opposite of a 'special deal'. (More of that in Chapter 19.)

In many respects it's a shame that there is a need for lawyers. It strikes me that they came into being because what people *thought* they had agreed wasn't what they had *actually* agreed. Or at least the aggrieved party had a different interpretation of the agreement. So the final step in negotiation has to be to tie up all the details. Write things down and ensure all the little add-ons are not left to assumptions.

Here is the summary of NEAT-NEAT negotiation:

- Never put a marker down first;
- Empathize;
- Ask about their interests;
- Think 'The other party needs to *think* they've done well';
- Neutralize your body;
- Equate everything in the deal;
- Agree only with a struggle; and
- Tie up all the details.

CHAPTER 12

Getting Commitment

In Chapter 10 we talked about closing being as easy as 'Will you marry me?' And there are three important issues about this analogy.

1   Without exception, all the women I surveyed told me that they *wanted* to be asked the question, 'Will you marry me?' They did not want their potential husband to just assume that marriage was a foregone conclusion. So asking for commitment is a good thing.
2   Good closing comes from good persuasion. And that means understanding the process.
3   Good persuasion comes from people who have developed a good relationship.

In Chapter 6 we looked at the first three principles of persuasion. We establish the other person's emotional needs by building the relationship. We ask questions, understand the implications, get to grips with the other person's point of view and always think long term. We talk about emotional value and not price. We make it easy for the other person to buy into our idea, product or service.

So far so good, but if we *only* do that we may finish up being seen as a nice guy. And nice guys, as Leo Duracher famously observed, 'come last'. The risk of just being seen as a nice guy is that you don't get the commitment. Selling (or persuading) without closing is like lathering without shaving.

A qualified prospect is like a good throw from the goalkeeper. Getting an appointment is like a good pass to the winger. An effective presentation is like a good cross. But if you don't put the ball in the onion bag, you don't score. It's just been nice to watch. There are no bonuses for nice football.

If you attempt to gain commitment or close too early, you run the risk of not establishing enough value for you or your product. Instead you may appear to have 'crashed' into the deal much as a Neanderthal would club an entire animal to death whenever he felt a little peckish. And sometimes you create irreparable damage just as our caveman did. Let's extend this Neanderthal analogy. In those days, there were two ways to get your food. You either went out hunter/gatherer style and clubbed the nearest prey without any thoughts on herd preservation or the ramifications for the animal; alternatively, you grew and harvested it at the time that nature allowed you to.

Nowadays there are arguably two ways of persuading. You either go out and club away by closing too early, or you grow and nurture the relationship much as a farmer sows his seeds, waters carefully and regularly, and waits for harvest time. The first approach *can* work and we'll look at how and when in a moment. The second also works so long as you can afford to wait. The analogy fails here because the skill of the salesman is to know when to 'club' and when to 'grow' – when to close and when to keep building the relationship and continue asking questions to establish the real needs.

The emotional needs.

In this third millennium people are more knowledgeable, more cynical and have more choice than ever before.

So what you need to be is what I call a 'burgeoner' (see Figure 12.1) – someone who can grow rapidly and flourish. Someone who can establish when to grow and when to close. Someone who knows how and why you need to develop the relationship, but just as importantly, when to ask for the commitment.

A 'no' from your prospect can mean one of four things:

1   you haven't developed the relationship enough;

2 you haven't developed the need;
3 the buyer just isn't sure yet; he doesn't have enough information; or
4 no.

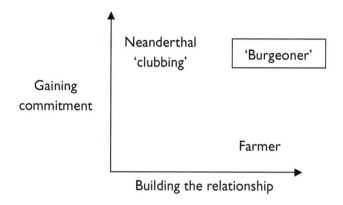

Figure 12.1 *Burgeoner I*

So a key lesson is not to confuse *your* situation with *his*. 'No' doesn't necessarily mean 'no'. You may have caught the person in the wrong mood and circumstance.

You need to build the relationship, and as you do so, look for when the time is right to ask for the commitment.

I am often asked: 'When do I close?' and the answer, as outlined in Chapter 10, is: 'When you are ready and have closed the gap between you and them.' But that is very different for different industries, isn't it?

If you have a straightforward, relatively low-cost sale and the buyer is in 'distress' (e.g. buying a new exhaust to get the car back on the road quickly), you can develop the relationship quickly and close quickly. Frankly, our Neanderthal friend can do the job. At least in the short term. If you are buying a washing machine when the old one has reached the end of its life and the washing is piling up, you can establish the needs quickly and often the buyer will close the sale himself. Our friendly receptionist in the hotel in Birmingham was doing a reasonable imitation of a Neanderthal clubman. And although he got the sale, he could have had more money and more chance of me returning if he had justified the price and shown a little more enthusiasm.

So to continue the analogy, if we replace the expression 'gaining commitment' with a sliding scale of 'easy sale' to 'complex sale', and substitute 'building the relationship' with a distress purchase at the low end and a complicated 'well thought through' buying decision at the high end of the scale, it looks like Figure 12.2.

The fact is, most of the people reading this book will want to persuade in the top right-hand segment of the last two matrices. And the more you are endeavouring to persuade someone to buy a product or service that is important to them – i.e. one that has repercussions well after you have gone *and* needs to be thought through – the more important the relationship. But also important is knowing when to close and when to ask for the commitment.

Things have moved on in business. People have wised up and buyers know more and more about 'closes'. The hoi polloi knows about marketing and 'positioning statements'. We recognize unsolicited mail, spam and free offers for trips abroad. Or at least we should. Scams still exist but we're a lot wiser. And an inappropriate closing technique can do more harm than good. The best close these days is something like, 'Are you happy that we've covered everything and would you like to go ahead?' Or simply, 'Would you like to go ahead?'

Basically, if you have developed the relationship in the right way and have established rapport, then the simple 'summary and shut up'

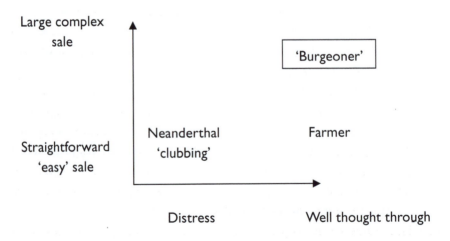

Figure 12.2 *Burgeoner 2*

will gain you the respect of the buyer and get you the commitment. You need to have your own words so it doesn't sound like you've learned a script. However, a simple, professional statement and question should be all that's needed if you have done the right things up to that point: 'So we have a product that meets your needs, is competitively priced, will help your efficiency and we can deliver with a full guarantee. Shall we go ahead and progress things straightaway?'

Importantly, I don't suggest '*Can* I go ahead and progress things?' This is about us, together, having worked as a team, deciding that this is the best thing to do. Say 'Shall we?', not 'Can I?'

The best closes come not only from developing the relationship and knowing when the gap is just about closed, but also *after* you have used a 'conditional close' or two. Expressions such as 'If I do this, can I assume we can go ahead?' or 'If I were able to respond to these three points to your satisfaction, can I assume we can go ahead?' should establish just how near you are to closing the gap.

When I work with buyers, they often want to know the different types of closes – as though they might be 'tricked' into buying. So if you are a student of closes, here are my Top Ten in alphabetical order:

1   The Alternative Close. 'Would you like it delivered Tuesday or Friday?' or, 'We can do the XL model in silver or we have the XLS in midnight blue – which one would you prefer?'

2   The Ego Close. 'We usually find that only the people who appreciate quality and are prepared to pay for the best service like this option. How do you feel about it?' 'Presumably cost wouldn't stop you from buying today ... would it?'

3   The Elimination Close. You list all the benefits and put a tick against all the issues you have addressed to the buyer's satisfaction. When you get to the one (or two) that is the reason for not going ahead, you highlight it and explain how you can overcome it and say, 'So we agree that if we can solve this one small issue we can go ahead? I know how we can do that so if I can use your phone and get clearance we can get started.'

4   The '50 Pence A Night' Close. This is a variant on the 'Power of One' we looked at earlier. I call it this because I was introduced

to it by Malcolm Newlyn who was the then marketing director of Dunlopillo beds. A bed is a major investment and he would say, 'I appreciate it's a lot of money but on average people have a bed for 12 years. Although it's just over £2000, that's only 50 pence per night. Wouldn't you pay 50 pence a night for a good night's sleep for the next twelve years?'

5   The 'Look At What You Could Have Had' Close (or 'Non-Buyer's Regret'). There was a popular TV programme in the 1970s called *Bullseye*. It was on every Sunday afternoon and the host was the Lancashire comedian, Jim Bowen. If the contestants had failed to win the mystery big prize he would always ask for the curtain to be pulled back to reveal the holiday or car or items of furniture and say, 'Look at what you could have won.' It was humiliating, but good viewing if you like that sort of thing. And an example of using it to sell televisions could be, 'The thing is, you don't want to be sitting at home knowing you could be watching the game on this big screen TV, do you?' In selling upgrades on airlines you could say, 'I wouldn't want you to be in economy not enjoying a night's sleep when you know that just 50 yards further up the plane they will be relaxing on those big seats.' (Ouch!)

6   The 'Price Goes Up On Monday' Close. If you are offering a special deal and can justify going back to the original price the following week, it's a good one to use but many people are wised up on this. It's old-fashioned and not one I suggest using unless it's a real situation. Where is your credibility when they *can* buy for the same price next week?

7   The Puppy Dog Close. Or, 'Let me leave it with you and you see how you get on with it.' If you work in retail, let people handle your product. Let them sit on it, try it on, feel it, hold it and stroke it. Imagine taking a puppy dog home and then the pet shop asking for it back a week later. Let your persuadee have the experience. It's why test drives work.

8   The Question Close. For example, if the persuading has been focused on saving money, a straightforward question such as, 'If you were ever going to start saving money when would be the best time to start?'

9 The 'Treat Yourself' Close. In many respects this fabulous close is the best example of why you shouldn't get towards the end of a presentation and simply 'pick' one of the ten closes. This one can be appropriate and very successful if you are selling a luxury product to an elderly person in his or her own home. Let's take the example of a stair lift. The elderly person is infirm, the product is within their price range and the stair lift will appreciably improve their standard of living. They are reluctant to buy only because they feel they are being decadent. They have had a lifetime of scrimping and saving and doing the best for their children, and to get them to commit the best close in this situation is to say, 'Treat yourself'. And shut up.

10 The Twenty Pound Note Close. When we worked with Leeds United the managing director was considering whether or not to spend money on advertising season tickets. In the previous years the case had been clear: basically, every £1 spent produced an extra £2 in income over and above renewals and what would have happened without advertising. I saw Bill in the Flying Pizza restaurant in north Leeds and went over to him. 'Hi Bill, can you give me £10?' I waited, he smiled and handed over a £10 note. I then took a £20 note from my pocket and gave it to him. 'That's what you're doing when you spend money with us, Bill.' And walked away. As we were having our cappuccinos he came over and gave us the go-ahead for the advertising. I didn't get the other £10 back but it was worth the investment.

Finally, I'd like to make reference to the 'just before I go' technique which can be used when you feel you have had a pretty definite 'no' and it's time to go. You begin to put your jacket on and say something like, 'I accept you're not going to buy from me today but just before I go can you tell me where I went wrong? Was it price? Was it quality? Was it something else?' Often when the buyer feels the pressure is off he will then tell you the real objection and you're back in business.

PART 4

People are Different

CHAPTER 13

Preparation

The key aspect of this chapter is preparation, and that, in turn, is about the foundation that you have to build on. When the foundation is one of friendship forged in the bar or on the golf course it's made of sand. It can be done, but the better you know someone the greater the expectation of him or her.

People behave in the way they want other people to behave. In a social situation people find it easier to have give and take than when there's money, ego and jobs on the line. Most of us live three lives. First, there's the life we live. The *real* life where you put the bins out for the bin men on a Sunday evening. Real life is mopping up your child's vomit; real life is having to buy the groceries and doing this under obligation rather than for desire. And then there's another life. That's the life we *want* to live. Call it aspiration. It's what we want for ourselves and our immediate family (or not). It's where we are heading in our dreams. It's the goals we have, regardless of how hard we are trying to achieve those goals.

And then there's the life we want other people to *think* we are living. Four hundred years ago in *As You Like It* the Bard wrote: 'All the world's a stage,/And all the men and women merely players:/They have their exits and their entrances;/And one man in his time plays many parts.' That's the life I'm talking about here. We play a part and we want people to think well of us (or ill). We want to project a certain image and so often that is not consistent with the life we are really living; with the real world we inhabit.

So when we 'act' in the social situation we create a certain impression of ourselves. And a commercial relationship built on the foundation and preparation of a social situation is likely to end in tears. In essence you don't get what's on the front page of the brochure. People are not what they appear to be. But sometimes we find ourselves in that lucky position of being able to make inadvertent use of a social relationship to benefit us commercially. Or at least, in this case, create a satisfying moment.

A friend of mine, Barry Smith, was financial director of Shires Bathrooms in the early 90s. I was always careful to separate my personal relationships from any possible commercial ones, and although as an agency we had targeted bathroom manufacturers as potential new clients, I hadn't mentioned it to Barry. We had done some substantial research into the bathroom market and undertaken group discussions. We had asked over 50 homeowners what they thought of magazine advertisements for the likes of Adamsez, Ideal Standard, Armitage Shanks, Plumb Center, Shires and Twyfords. I had written to the managing directors, marketing directors and marketing managers of these companies and explained that they could have the research for free on three conditions. Firstly, that they had to meet me face-to-face, secondly that they would listen to 15 minutes on the agency's capabilities and thirdly that the meeting would be at our offices rather than theirs.

All but one were happy to comply. It was a simple case of each client understanding the rules. They got free research and we got to meet them so that if they were to become unhappy with their agency we might be considered. And, on the grounds that we had commissioned the research, we could tell each client about the reactions of consumers not only to their advertising but also to that of their competitors.

The one that didn't want to meet me was Charles – the marketing manager of Shires. I still to this day don't know why but the irony was that Shires' advertising was universally disliked. It was bottom of the pile. The reasons were easy to see. So I went on a bit of a crusade to get Charles to come to the agency and he eventually, albeit reluctantly, agreed to come one Thursday morning.

By chance I was having a beer with Barry at a Round Table night on the Wednesday evening. He asked how business was and who I was seeing and, frankly, I couldn't help myself but tell him I was meeting up with his marketing manager. And he told me that they were mightily unimpressed by the response figures they had been getting in the likes of the *Sunday Times*, the *Daily Telegraph* and the *Mail on Sunday*. He asked me what sort of response figures could be expected in those publications and went on to tell me the response they had actually had in the previous week's papers.

So when Charles came in the next day, boy was I prepared! He was very offhand and took our reporting of the feedback to the Shires ads badly. So badly that he became very defensive and said that if I was such an expert what sort of response did I think last weekend's ads achieved in – you've guessed it – the *Sunday Times, Daily Telegraph* and *Mail on Sunday*?

I am not making this up!

So I gave him an 'estimate'. I told him what I thought was a reasonable range, and then delivered the killer blow by 'guessing' (I didn't keep them precise) what response he probably got from the three ads in question.

Are you familiar with the expression 'ashen faced?'

Now, we didn't win the account for all sorts of reasons but boy, was he impressed! And although it's a rare opportunity to know that sort of information, that's the ideal preparation for a meeting, isn't it?

So what can *you* do to ensure you are *prepared* to be persuasive? Well, having now covered the essence of the persuasion process, we can more easily talk about preparation.

It's not just anticipating the persuadee's needs and reading up but also about thinking things through. It's what I call the 'Ball Boy Factor'.

I had the idea that potential clients who were into football would love to play a game alongside their heroes. I knew the former England captain Trevor Cherry quite well and asked if he could fix up some players. So with Joe Corrigan in goal, Trevor at centre half and Frank Worthington up front I was to captain a side against an opposition eleven that included former players Eddie Gray, Derek Parlane and Arthur Graham. I wanted to play the game at Accrington Stanley's ground. It had been made famous by a TV commercial for milk and it was only an hour's drive away. Keith Hackett agreed to referee the match and so I wrote invitations to a group of clients and potential clients; a bunch of excited businessmen who are then able to have a distinctly memorable time and feel a certain obligation to us.

I had already spoken to the people at Accrington Stanley and they had agreed to let us use the pitch, dressing rooms and all the facilities. But in order to complete my preparation I wanted to visit the stadium. The secretary of the club couldn't understand why; we had all the arrangements in force and he saw no need for me to visit in advance. But I knew that to be properly prepared I needed to go. The first reason, which I couldn't share with him, was that I never assumed people would do what they said they were going to do; and the second was what became known as the 'Ball Boy Factor'.

He toured me round the dressing rooms and I realized then I hadn't thought about providing tie-ups. As we journeyed round it occurred to me only then that I should provide shampoo and remind the players to bring their own towels and so on. It was when we were walking around the pitch he asked if I wanted ball boys.

Of course! It's a huge ground and would have next to no one in the stands. Without ball boys we would be forever jumping over the barrier and running up the terraces to retrieve the ball. And frankly, I couldn't see Joe Corrigan doing that every time someone skied one over his crossbar. At £5 each, I booked four and it made all the difference. As is always the case, the evening's success relied on the little things being right. Similarly your ability to persuade in a meeting relies on you preparing fully and getting the little things right.

Nick Faldo always pulls slightly at the crease on his trousers before he takes a putt; Tim Henman bounces the tennis ball two or three times before he serves; footballers place the ball themselves before taking a penalty. Indeed, all the people at the top of their sport have fixed routines that they follow in order to get into the right frame of mind.

Do you?

When you enter the reception area before a meeting, do you prepare mentally? Do you always go to the toilet to check your appearance or just assume your tie is fastened straight? Do you carry shoe-cleaning brushes with you? Do you always use a mouth spray before you meet your client or customer? Do you check you have a spare pen in case the one you have doesn't work? Do you have a small hairbrush in your bag or briefcase or handbag? Do you double-check the names of the people you are seeing before you knock on the proverbial door?

Or is it too much trouble?

Do you know what sort of person you are meeting? Do they want it quick and snappy or do they want to chat? I have a number of agents who represent me. One of the distinctive features about my marketing is that I write long letters to them. I don't expect them to read it all – the essence of the letter is always in the subheads and the PS so you don't need to read the whole thing. But one agent, Brendan Barns, e-mailed me and said, 'I'm sure there is some strategy to your approach here but have to confess I rather prefer brevity.' So I write pithy one-pagers to Brendan.

Decorators, tilers, carpet fitters and tradesmen of all types tell me that preparation is critical. Engineers tell me that the size of the hole in the ground dictates how high they can build their buildings. Chefs tell me that preparing the food is the most important aspect of cooking. Motorcyclists tell me that maintaining and preparing the engine and being ready for the ride are critical. Nurses tell me that without cleaning a wound properly, it doesn't heal. Farmers tell me that if they don't sow seeds in the right way at the right time, their harvest isn't maximized.

And so on.

Preparation is about doing ordinary things well. Little things like establishing how long the meeting will last and who'll be there, confirming the appointment in writing, gathering all the information that you need and letting them know discreetly that you have prepared. It flatters them. It says to the recipient that this is an important meeting. It's about preparing to meet their expectations; it's about doing all you can to avoid being late. It's about knowing all that you can about the internal politics and attitudes, competitors and existing supply arrangements, the trading preferences of the prospect, and so on.

CHAPTER 14

Different Strokes for Different Folks

My old Uncle John used to say, 'All the world's queer save thee and me – and even thee's a little queer.' People are funny, aren't they? They're different. I am a fan of Myers Briggs and a whole host of personality profiling systems. I have a passing interest in astrology. I read books where people are segmented into animals such as sharks, tigers, puppies and bears. NLP practitioners talk about auditory, visual and kinaesthetic types. You can segment people as either positive or negative versus active and passive. And neatly put everyone on the planet into one of four 'types'. Positive and active people have a dynamic effect on you. Positive and passive people are good at detail and are hard working, whereas negative and active folk are trouble! They're disruptive and not constructive. Keep away from them. Particularly the ones who stay in their pyjamas all day. And finally there are the 'negative and passives' – they suck the life out of you slowly. (The 'anti-cyclones' of misery!)

I haven't finished yet. There is a 'system' of establishing whether people are 'activists, reflectors, theorists or pragmatists'. Another whereby people are either technical expert/analytical, bottom liners, friendly supporter/amiable or extrovert. Then there's left and right brain dominance. Left brain equals learning such as language and logical mathematical processes, whilst right brain equals rhyme, rhythm and pictures. And let's not forget our favourite; the socio-economic groupings A, B, C1, C2, D and E.

And all this is without touching on some of the neat acronyms that advertising agencies have come up with such as Glams (grey, leisured, affluent and married), Yuppies (young urban professionals), Oilkies (one income, loads of kids) and Dinkies (double income, no kids).

According to one anthropologist you can make judgements on people by the size of the peel in somebody's marmalade. I can quite believe it.

Where will it all end? They all have a role but none of them have the answer. The real answer is that we are all different. Now if the key to persuasion is seeing things from the other person's point of view, there has to be more to it than simply saying someone is an ENTJ (Extended iNtuitive Thinking Judger; a Myers-Briggs personality type term), left brain dominant, 'B', extrovert, negative Libra who prefers shredless marmalade! People's propensity to be persuaded is influenced not only by their need for what it is you are offering but also their childhood, their experience in similar situations and what their peers and bosses expect of them. People buy emotionally and justify logically. And what you offer typically has what might be described as hard differentiators (logic) and soft differentiators (emotion).

Logical (hard differentiators) is the tip of iceberg.

Logic is what you appear to want and what you say you want. Cost, speed, size, compatibility, reliability, specification etc.

Emotion is ego, kudos, power, politics, chemistry, security, CV building, effect on other people, how it will reflect on your management, your own 'brand reputation', image, relationships and so on. And most of this stuff your buyer either doesn't know (it's in his subconscious) or doesn't want to know.

And there isn't one 'process' we all follow, is there? Sometimes we start with a basic need for a product or service. We then decide what we want and the 'process' can be reasonably logical at this point. But then we get into our higher needs – our emotional needs. Sometimes we buy things we don't need. Sometimes we buy things we didn't know we needed until we saw them.

In addition to all that, if you are selling in business-to-business (B2B), you have more than one person involved. Why do people buy in B2B? Well, once a need has been established (and over and above their need to be certain that the new product or service will be sustainable, reliable and good value), there are typically four reasons to buy:

1   it saves or makes them money;
2   it saves time;
3   it improves efficiency or their ability to compete; and
4   it makes life easier and allows them to do other things.

Within this, the top management typically are most interested in the return on investment. They want knowledge and they want numbers. They want improvement and that means money. As we said earlier, don't talk to the big cheese until you can talk numbers.

But the department head is often more focused on the solution to a problem. When I got potential clients away from their office and asked them what they *really* wanted from an agency, they would confide in me that what they often wanted – their real, emotional need – was a solution for an easier life. They didn't necessarily want the best price. They had to be *seen* to be getting and asking for the best price, but the main focus was on protecting their job and allowing them to do what they wanted to do. What of the technical people? They need technical evidence; they want reassurance not only on the technical ability but also on back-up. They sometimes want the latest 'toy' and who cares about the money – that's someone else's department.

How 'big' is the purchase? If words are the language of the relatively low-cost items you buy in a retail shop, numbers are the language of the B2B 'large ticket' sale. So if you are selling to a group of people, I recommend that you 'plot' them on the scale in Figure 14.1.

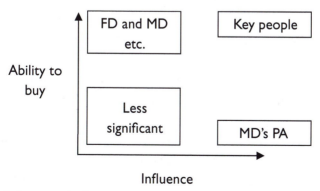

Figure 14.1 *Buyers and influencers*

The horizontal axis is the individual's ability to influence the decision and the vertical scale the ability to actually buy. Do you recall in Chapter 9 Sebastian and I buying the VW Polo? We examined who could influence and who could buy. My wife had a big influence and could also buy. I could buy as I was ultimately the one with the cheque book, but Seb could influence enormously. He had power of veto. No money; loads of power. And although he didn't *see* his power of veto, it was important for me (the 'managing director' in this case) to not only have him along in the decision, but also allow him to influence part of the decision so that he would be more interested in looking after and maintaining the car. It wasn't a decision 'foisted' on him. In the Victorian era that's how decisions were made. In the 21st century later we need to be more conciliatory.

So plot the people you are seeing. By all means plot them as activists or pragmatists, ENTJs and left brainers. But more importantly don't miss out on who can make decisions and who can influence. And establish their individual needs if you want to be successful.

I shared an office with my PA for 20 years. My relationship with her was important to me because the success of that relationship had a huge bearing on my ability to do the thing that I was best at – getting in front of potential clients. And if anyone who wished to sell to me was rude to her, I found out about it pretty much instantly. That then made *their* job very difficult indeed. Partly because she was my gatekeeper and partly because I didn't want to put broken glass into all the layers of tissue paper I was laying down between her and me. Could she 'buy'? No. Could she influence my relationship and thereby willingness to buy from that rude supplier? You bet.

So *plot* the people you're seeing, establish and list their different emotional needs. Reinforce the things you can do better than your competitors, work on the issues you're struggling on and remember these five things.

1   They buy to solve a pain or fulfil a desire (carrot and stick). The key to getting the sale is to move the prospect's *pain* (his or her NAIL) to the top of his or her list. And to do that you need to be

persistent. You need them to experience or at least *see* the pain of *not* making a decision.

2   People buy emotionally and justify logically.

3   All the people who can influence and/or buy have different needs. Different strokes for different folks.

4   The conversation *is* the relationship, so the depth of your questioning and the depth of your conversation *is* the depth of relationship.

5   You need to ask good questions of each individual. You have to feel how they are feeling about what's important to them. Ask the hard questions and deal with the responses.

Why do people buy anyway? Time for Chapter 15.

Why do People Buy Things?

People buy because they have a need, right? Well, yes they do, but why do they buy one brand over another? Why do they prefer one colour to another, or a particular retailer? And what about impulse purchases? What goes on there?

Why do we spend more than we have to? Your decision to buy *everything* that you buy is influenced by the thoughts impressed on your subconscious mind through a set of beliefs that you have developed. When you set out to buy, your conscious mind is the starter, but after that it's the subconscious mind that is the motor; the driver. Just as you didn't consciously decide what you think of someone when you first met him or her, similarly you are not in full control when you are deciding what to buy.

People are more likely to buy when they are in an 'emotional' state; that is to say, the 'right frame of mind'. People buy when they are in a state of 'trouble' or tremendous opportunity. 'Emotion', mood and circumstance are all factors in how we buy what we buy and in this chapter we look at it from a psychological point of view. Consumers in a good mood will be more aware of positive attributes of a product or service than those who are sad, angry or resentful at the time you are trying to persuade them. Indeed, attempting to get closure from someone in the wrong frame of mind can irritate.

I worked with a sales representative – a lady called Margaret – in Cheshire one day. We were going to see a vet and, as we waited in the reception, we could hear the raised voice of a man who was unhappy – extremely unhappy – about the bill he had received for treating his

Rottweiler. And the Rottweiler was there. And he was getting upset too.

What a noise! I was literally frightened of what might happen to Margaret and I should the dog get even more agitated. When the angry man left I asked myself if there was any point at all in talking about a new drug to a vet who had been in such an ordeal. Margaret did absolutely the right thing in making tea and biscuits and sympathizing with the vet in that situation.

The result? No sale then (there wasn't going to be one anyway unless the vet's need was desperate) but for next time the relationship had been built. Tissue paper well and truly in the box. No room for the Neanderthal at that point.

Dickson & Sawyer did some comprehensive and profoundly interesting research on supermarket shopping. They concluded that although shoppers *said* they looked at competitor brands and made price comparisons, observational techniques clearly illustrated that:

- they did not check prices;
- more than half did not know what they had paid; and
- regular buyers did not even know that their preferred product was on special offer.

The conclusion? *We don't know what we're doing!*

Why did we buy into that cultural thing that happened in the 1960s, when artists such as Bob Dylan, John Lennon, Joan Baez and Mick Jagger made a difference to us? Why did we believe in the Age of Aquarius, Che Guevara and Flower Power? What was the mystique that was right for that time and not for now?

Why do respectable middle-aged men buy Harley Davidsons and drive through sleepy villages on a Sunday morning looking 'hard'? Or is *that* the reason?

Why do people go fishing? Is it the fish they're really after or is the peace and quiet, and the mental challenge?

After winning one particular account in the advertising agency I asked the client, Geoff Thompson, why he had chosen us over and above the competition. 'You were all pretty much the same. We just thought we'd have more fun with you guys.'

A young woman working for the Children's Society stopped me in the street in Knightsbridge recently. It was 5 p.m. on a warm spring evening and I had just finished the first day of a two-day course. She had such a passion for what she was doing. Her eyes glowed as she told me what good work the Society were undertaking to help children who were being abused 'as we speak'. There was no intention before I met her of committing myself to £10 a month to play my small part but that's what happened.

Why did I buy? Did I have a need? Well, if I did, I didn't know about it before she approached me. Do I still pay the £10 a month? Yes.

In Chapter 10 we looked at buyer's regret and cognitive dissonance; the very fact they exist tells us that we don't simply buy what we need when we need it. We can be persuaded: sometimes by others in the case of this excellent young woman in London, and sometimes by ourselves or friends and relatives we are with. We will look at peer pressure and at all the various reasons why people buy.

Why they buy people, products, services, even excuses.

In Chapter 5 we looked at the 'Triangle of Relationships' and how we move from ritual and cliché. The relationships we have all around us sit in this triangle. We have a small number of very close friends with whom we have a 'peak' relationship and a limited number of people with whom we discuss our feelings. The number of people with whom we have a 'ritual and cliché' relationship is literally too many to count.

Now let's relate that triangle to how we buy jewellery as a gift (see Figure 15.1). Let's assume that a man is buying jewellery for a woman. Why he is buying is going to influence how and what he buys, and a good jeweller establishes the 'why' before the 'what'.

Here are five possible 'positionings' for our buyer.

1   Our buyer is coming from the bottom of the triangle and trying to impress a new belle.
2   He is in a developing relationship and looking to gain progress up the triangle.

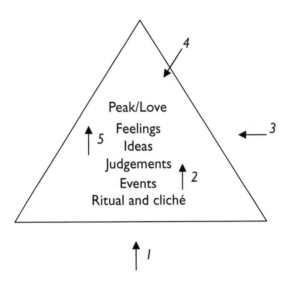

Figure 15.1 *Buying positions*

3   He is attempting to get out of the dog house – he has been kicked out of the triangle! – and back into the relationship.
4   He is having an illicit and short-term affair and therefore attempting to go straight in at the top and straight back out again.
5   It is a solution to a problem – Christmas, birthday, anniversary, etc.

For our persuadee, isn't it so much better to know the real *need* before we start to provide solutions?

The fact is you have behaved your way into a problem you need to behave your way out of it.

And life stage has a huge bearing on persuasion too.

If you don't know about Maslow, let me précis his life and work. Abraham Harold Maslow was born on 1 April 1908 in New York. He was the first of seven children born to Jewish, immigrant parents from Russia. Maslow created the now famous 'hierarchy of needs'. The essence of his hierarchy is that you cannot focus on other issues if your physiological needs are not catered for. At its most basic level this includes oxygen, water and food, as well as the need to sleep, avoid pain and so on.

If those basic needs are catered for, you can begin to focus on safety and security needs. You naturally become increasingly interested in stability and protection for you and your immediate family. Living in a safe neighbourhood, having job security and a retirement plan, that sort of thing.

Once you feel comfortable that you can provide for your family and feel secure, then you feel a greater need for friends and sound relationships. Or what Maslow called 'Love and Belonging'. It was interesting to see how many people became more interested in rugby when England won the World Cup in 2003. A great sense of belonging can only be there if you share the interest. During the football tournament I referred to in Chapter 11, 'White Van Man' was everywhere with his little flag of St George fluttering from his aerial and window.

And then we look for self-esteem. At one level, the respect of others: status, fame, recognition, reputation and so on. At another level, the need for self-respect, confidence, competence, achievement, independence, and freedom.

If your aspiring career is under threat, you slip down the 'greasy pole' and want attention. If your partner announces they are having an affair and are leaving you, it seems that love is again all you ever wanted. And it works for nations too. When society itself struggles, people look for a strong leader.

Maslow died in 1970 at the age of 62, and as you would expect, others have developed his work. After all, things have moved on since his original idea was published in 1954. And it's that development that is useful to help us understand why people buy certain things in today's economic climate. In the UK in the early 1950s there was still rationing after the war, there were few brands, relatively little advertising and life was lived at a slower pace than today. Indeed, some of the priorities of today's youth look rather fanciful to those born before the mid-1950s with money to spend and still having the values of being brought up in the 1960s.

Maslow importantly pointed out the need for air, food, water, shelter and so on. But there's another important aspect in retail. Showing people how much you care isn't just something you say, something you feel, but also something you *do*. As a married man who sometimes has to accompany his wife on shopping trips that include looking at ladies' dresses, what I really, really, really want is a chair.

A chair in a retail shop says that they care about me. Most men tell me that after about 45 minutes of looking at ladies' dresses they begin to lose the will to live, but a chair and a newspaper can extend that period substantially. So why don't ladies' dress shops quite get it?

Of course, Maslow failed to touch on one or two other things apart from the seating arrangements in dress shops. It strikes me that not only do blokes out shopping with their wives want to sit down a lot, the degree of indebtedness they feel towards their partner is directly linked to the length of their relationship. Naturally, when this is at an early stage both are keen to please the other, particularly in the bedroom. However, as the relationship matures, sex is often reserved for special occasions such as to celebrate a British gold medal at the Olympics or the installation of a new Pope. The conclusion? The longer the relationship, the less interested and indebted the person and the greater the need to sit down in dress shops.

Right; got that off my chest. Back to Maslow.

It is clear that 'esteem needs' are greater for today's youth than ever before and that brands matter. As we get older we search for knowledge and meaning – what Maslow calls 'cognitive needs'. Importantly, as we become more wealthy, it is an appreciation of (and search for) beauty and balance that means we pay for works of art and look for just the right dress for the occasion – 'aesthetic needs'.

When Bono wants to help play his part in reducing Third World debt, when Sting wants to help stop the destruction of rain forests in South America, they are both seeking to realize their personal potential and find true fulfilment. They are seeking personal growth and peak experiences.

'Self-actualization needs' are about helping others to achieve self-actualization. And on that warm spring day on Knightsbridge, I was giving money to charity because of a deep feeling of needing to 'do my bit'.

So what motivates us? Allow me to make reference to another American academic – David McClelland.

David Clarence McClelland (1917–98) achieved his doctorate in psychology at Yale in 1941 and became professor at Wesleyan University. He then taught and lectured, including a spell at Harvard from 1956, where he studied motivation and the need people have for achievement. He pioneered workplace motivational thinking, and talked about three quite different 'needs' – achievement, authority and affiliation.

He argued that some people are 'achievement motivated' and therefore seek achievement, attainment of realistic but challenging goals, and advancement in the job. There is a strong need for feedback with them as to achievement and progress, and a need for a sense of accomplishment.

Others feel the need for authority and power. These people are 'authority motivated' and need to be influential, effective and to make an impact. There is a strong need to lead and for their ideas to prevail. There is also motivation and need towards increasing personal status and prestige. The point is, if you manage one of these people and don't give them enough 'rope', they become frustrated and disruptive, and may even leave.

And a third section (there are more) are the 'affiliation motivated'. These people have a need for friendly relationships and are motivated towards interaction with other people. The affiliation driver produces motivation and the need to be liked and held in popular regard. These people are team players. They're great to have around and be around, but don't isolate them or they won't be at their best.

As with all the other classifications we discussed in Chapter 14, most people possess and exhibit a combination of these characteristics. So why do some people buy into your ideas and others not? Why do people buy things? Well, not only do we have all these factors into play, we also need to consider mood and circumstance and the fact that we're not in control of 95% of our thoughts!

Many men don't know the size of their own underpants. As my eldest said to me a little while ago, 'They're funny blokes, women.' This book is not dedicated to the difference between men and women but if you can explain it all to everyone, please send up a flare.

We are enormously influenced by touching things. We often need to talk to a friend, colleague or sales assistant just to allow ourselves to vocalize and rationalize the need to buy. Particularly towels, bed linen, carpets, children's pushchairs and, of course, hammers. It's a bloke thing.

I am at the Great Yorkshire Show. It is an annual event and stallholders are many and varied. As I am walking along one of the avenues I see the SkyTV stand and walk in. We have been unhappy with cable TV for sometime and I'm conscious that dealing direct with Sky can offer us benefits that we don't currently enjoy. My sons tell me it's a 'no brainer' but I haven't done it.

So Jon from Cardiff approaches me and asks me what I'm interested in. I explain my situation and he chats me through the benefits. He allows me to hold the remote control and see for myself just how easy it is to record programmes, pause live TV if the phone rings and use the other interactive services. I'm still waiting for the device that allows you to pause individuals for 90 minutes while the match is on, but other than that, I think it's great.

And I buy.

The whole thing is all over within ten minutes but I buy because mood and circumstance are right and I am able to have someone listen to me. It is a rare opportunity to speak to a specialist *(rarity)*, he is a likeable guy *(empathy)*, he is an *authority* on the subject, there is a *special deal* on at this particular time and he is going to such trouble and listens to me so intently that I feel obliged *(obligation)*. I am relieved that my youngest son won't yet again chastise me for having done nothing about it *(nervousness)* and, importantly, other people around me are buying *(social pressure)*.

And that's why I bought. I had seven reasons. Time for the final acronym. There are seven psychological reasons for why we buy anything and everything. You rarely need all of them but you always need at least one of them. REASONS is an acronym that spells out those key psychological triggers; Rarity, Empathy and Ego, Authority, Special Deal, Obligation, Nervousness and Social Pressure.

Frankly, buying, shopping, committing to a decision is something we ourselves need to know more about. Time for Chapter 16.

PART 5

Why People Buy What They Buy

Rarity

About six or seven months after we set up Advertising Principles, I decided it would be a neat idea to provide free bacon sandwiches for all the staff on pay day. No money, just a bacon buttie. Only kidding. People were paid by bank transfer on the last Thursday of the month so there was no 'pay cheque' or cash to count. And for no other reason that I thought it was a nice thing to do, I asked my PA to buy 27 bacon sandwiches, and we put a Tannoy out that at 10 a.m. on pay day there would be a free bacon sandwich for everyone.

Which went down well.

After a couple of months my PA started getting a call or two on the day before pay day with requests. 'Can I have sausage and tomato and can David have his bacon well done?' 'Can we have two egg sandwiches and one plain toast?'

Which was fine.

After six months had passed, it became something of a chore for my PA. Few simply settled for the bacon sandwich and were putting in their orders. Slips of paper and phone calls built up to the point that there were more 'specials' than bacon butties.

One pay day I went down to reception and found one of the young female account executives in what can only be referred to as a 'right state'.

'Not again! You can't get anything done round here. I ask for egg and there's never any egg left – it's terrible.'

I stopped the bacon sandwiches then. It wasn't 'special'. And once that happened and it became a 'given', the whole psychology changed.

Dr Terry Pettijohn, a social psychologist at Mercyhurst College in Pennsylvania, carried out a study involving examining photographs of actresses and pored over issues of *Playboy* magazine to see whether there was a correlation between attraction and national prosperity. 'Boom or bust' then took on a whole new meaning. The clear conclusion from studying faces and figures of 'Playmates of the Year' from 1960 to 2000 was that men prefer stronger-looking women in hard times, and softer, more vulnerable types when things are buoyant. In essence, we want someone to have fun with when times are good, and we want someone to take care of us – and themselves – when times are bad. Pettijohn created an annual 'hard times measure' by tracking changes in US statistics on unemployment, marriage, homicide and other factors for the years 1960 to 2000.

Then, using clear, front-on photographs of *Playboy* Playmates of the Year for each of those 40 years, his researchers made precise measurements of key face and body dimensions.

Comparing models over the years, the researchers discovered that, in hard times, Playmates tended to be slightly older, heavier and taller, with larger waists and bigger waist-to-hip ratios. Smaller eyes – a feature linked to 'stronger' faces – were also predominant.

The boom years of the early 1960s, for example, produced both the youngest-ever Playmate of the Year (18-year-old Donna Michelle, 1964) and the lightest (102-pound June Cochran, 1963), according to Pettijohn.

It was also in the 'Swinging Sixties' that Audrey Hepburn and Twiggy were at the height of their popularity, whereas in the early 1990s, when the economic picture was relatively gloomy, it was the heavyweight actresses such as Emma Thompson and Kate Winslet that were getting the meatier roles. If Dawn French ever makes it big in Hollywood, my advice is to liquidate your assets fast.

In summary, when times are good and there is plenty of food around, an attractive woman is a slim one. When times are bad in poor countries, an attractive woman is a plump one.

Basically, we want what we can't have.

We want something that's special. It's what I call the 'tiramisu factor'. I like tiramisu. It's very tasty. But if I had it every night I would tire of it and eventually grow to dislike it.

It was whilst doing research on food and people's attitudes to it that I began to realize that we are all looking for the perfect food. Great taste *and* good for you.

Does it exist? Can we have chocolate lager that doesn't pile on the pounds? It seems that foods are on a sliding scale shown in Figure 16.1.

Basically, if it tastes great it's not good for you and if it's good for you it tastes like cod liver oil. There are some mid-ground products that sit in the middle of 'life's food plan' such as milk, orange juice and fish, but food manufacturers are all looking for the Holy Grail – really tasty and no guilt. Hence the success of a whole range of products that offer the consumer the opportunity to buy in the top left-hand corner of the matrix.

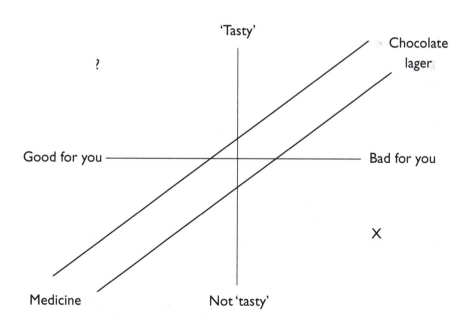

Figure 16.1 *'Food, glorious food'*

We are drawn to things that are rare. The more difficult things are to have – indeed the more we are told we can't have them – the more we want them. The forbidden fruit. The expression 'play hard to get' summarizes it.

As a family going to Disneyland in Florida, we originally planned to have seven days there, but opted to stay longer to see more of the park and experience more of the rides. I clearly remember my youngest son on the tenth day saying with a weary expression, 'I'm all Disneyed out, dad.' He had had too much of a good thing.

Think of paintings that are signed by the artist. 1 of 100 or 13 of 500. They are worth more. Why? Because they are rare and special.

I was buying a small sculpture recently and asked the owner of the gallery why one piece – which looked very much like another – was appreciably more expensive. 'Ah,' he said, turning each, in turn, upside down so I could see the detail on the bottom of the sculptures, 'this one is one of only twenty the sculptor made, whereas this one is one of 40.' And that was all the explanation he felt he needed to make – one was rarer than the other!

Do you recall the Joni Mitchell song, 'Big Yellow Taxi'? In it she sings, 'You don't know what you got till it's gone'.

Rarity.

It was around the same time that the song 'Je T'aime' was banned by the BBC. Needless to say it then went to number one! Children under 18 want to go to movies with an '18' classification. Under-age drinkers want to do just that. Philatelists tell me that postage stamps with errors are appreciably more valuable. And the Penny Black is worth a lot more than a Penny Red. Why? It's rarer. People want more of what they can have less of and less of what they can have a lot of.

So how can you use this?

I did some work for a very nice restaurant in town. A friend of mine, Bob Fern, owned it. Bob needed more people in his restaurant and we put together a special deal that offered a great menu and a free half bottle of wine. We organized an insert in the local paper and bookings started coming in. I had already said there needed to be an 'end date' on the offer as part of the rarity factor. ('Closing down sale',

'Only one left', 'We're running out of stock' and 'I can squeeze you in' are all exploiting this psychological need).

In a matter of days Bob was full on Friday and Saturday nights.

He called me.

'What should I do, Phil? I'm full every Friday and Saturday. Shall I extend the offer?' I suggested he tell people he was full on Friday and Saturday even when he wasn't but he could offer them a table mid-week. 'But I'm half empty mid-week.' I asked him if he wanted to be part of an experiment and he agreed. We would hold our nerve and tell people we were full. The offer was too good to extend but he had availability mid-week. Guess what? Yes, he started filling up mid-week. Marvellous! People want more of what they can have less of and less of what they can have a lot of.

I worked for a guy called Jerome Hirst in the mid-1980s. He was chairman of a now-defunct advertising agency, The AB Group. I was with him one day when he got a phone call from a client. Could they have lunch? Jerome opened his diary and said to the client, 'Let's see what I can do that particular week. I've got a diary like the Paris Metro.' It was empty save for the hand-written note, 'Pay rates bill'.

I am not making this up!

He gave the impression to the client that to have lunch with such a busy man was almost a privilege. One of the ironies of the way I now make a living is that clients want to be able to book me on the date of their choice but would be horrified if I were always available as that would mean I had no bookings.

Work that one out.

The question for you is, can you make your product or service seem rarer and more special? Toy manufacturers often get it down to a fine art at Christmas. We caring parents want to buy that special toy for our youngster, and the more difficult it is to buy, the more the child wants it. Have you ever seen children want to play with the same toy over and over, despite the fact there are plenty of other toys to play with?

And rarity comes in different guises. There are more than three, but here are what I believe to be the key aspects of rarity.

- Old or extinct (what you can't have). The antiques business is probably the finest example of using 'old rarity'. Chippendale can only have made so many pieces, so their cost increases if popularity remains high.

    Often, singers/songwriters are far more popular after their untimely death than they ever were before. Think Buddy Holly, Eva Cassidy, Eddie Cochrane, Janis Joplin, Marc Bolan, Jimi Hendrix, Jim Morrison, Tim Hardin, Steely Dan's and The Beach Boys' drummers, half of the Grateful Dead (very grateful I should imagine), Patsy Kline, Sam Cooke, Brian Jones, Sid Vicious and, of course, John Lennon and Elvis. Even The Carpenters weren't safe. The most popular method of premature death in the glory days of rock 'n' roll were drugs, suicide and plane crashes. A fair number died in their own swimming pools and even more died in their own vomit. Picking up a guitar or a drum kit in the early 1970s was more risky that going to Lenin Square with a sawn-off shotgun and letting everyone know what you thought of Karl Marx. Why Sam Cooke didn't just stay in his motel room and why John Denver isn't revered I don't know.

    Fawlty Towers might not have proved quite so popular if there had been 130 episodes rather than 12. Even *Friends* knew that you could only have so much of a good thing. The very last episode was watched by a huge audience because it had become suddenly rare. Enoch Powell said, 'All political lives, unless they are cut off in midstream at a happy juncture, end in failure because that is the nature of politics and human affairs.' Familiarity eventually breeds contempt and people tire of anything that is *too* familiar.

- New (what you can't have right now). Car manufactures use this very well. Often they hold back stock so that they can hold their top price as the new car is exclusive, prestigious and 'rare'. We are told by the salesman that they are 'difficult to get hold of'. Cars are released in line with demand but, importantly, just lagging behind it.

- Not allowed (what you can't have because of the 'rules'). I was running an open course in London recently and we were talking about the use of rarity. A head teacher of a well-known public school was a delegate and asked if he could tell a story. He went on to tell us that the most effective advertisement he had ever run in a national newspaper he did so by mistake. The school was fully subscribed and there was a waiting list for some years. He had a small but steady stream of people calling and asking if their son or daughter could apply, and it was proving an irritant, as there were no spaces. So he decided to run an advertisement in a national newspaper to simply say that the school was full. Effectively, 'Please don't call us – the answer is no.' He was then, to use his own expression, 'inundated' with response! People want what they can't have. They also want what everybody else has got if it's the best and we'll come to that later. Think ticket touts at major sporting events.

Think invitations to the Queen's garden parties. Indeed, think of our own Honours' List. Many people are desperately keen to have an MBE or OBE because relatively few people have them – and they can't be bought! If I were advising parents of teenage children I would suggest they be cautious about completely forbidding their children to drink, smoke and see friends they themselves regard as unsavoury. Weren't Adam and Eve banished from the Garden of Eden because they craved the one thing that God said they couldn't have – the forbidden fruit?

Welcome to rarity.

The lesson for you? Can you highlight unique benefits and exclusive information? Can you make you, your product or service seem more 'rare' and 'special'?

CHAPTER 17

Empathy and Ego

You know those people who buy things they don't need with money they haven't got to impress people they don't like? We're complicated creatures, aren't we?

As I mentioned in Chapter 3, I've spent a few happy Saturdays and Sundays in autumn taking my sons to university. Without planning it I wear pretty much what every other dad is wearing. As the dads walk past each other we all acknowledge each other with a nod of the head and the briefest of 'hellos' that we are 'alike'. We are doing the same thing and therefore we have empathy. The students grunt acknowledgement too, but mums and dads don't greet students and vice versa. People buy brands because of the emotional appeal. People buy emotionally and justify logically, remember? It explains the passion of a sports fan rooting for 'their' team; the importance of having a common goal and why we buy on impulse.

We have empathy.

In the 1960s there were mods and rockers and hippies. I was a bit too young to fully appreciate the '60s, but I caught the back end of them. In the summer of '69 I got a part-time job and bought myself brogues, a pair of Stay Press trousers, a Ben Sherman button-down shirt and a corduroy Wrangler jacket. Brown it was, and I only ever fastened the one button near the top. With a short haircut I was a mod. But I also had a motorbike because I saw Peter Fonda in *Easy Rider* and thought he was the coolest dude on the planet. I had a 250cc Ariel Arrow. I painted stars and stripes on the petrol tank, fitted ape hanger handle bars and completed the ensemble with a chrome back rest and a bit of fur on the top.

I must have looked a right wazzock.

I also learned that I couldn't wear the mod gear with the bike. Fellow mods didn't like the bike and rockers couldn't get the gear I was wearing. No empathy with anyone.

I was in Bantry Bay in south-west Ireland a few years ago at a music festival. A relatively unknown artist was playing and in introducing the next singer-songwriter, he said 'And please welcome a West County Cork boy …' And the crowd went wild. He was one of them. They had common ground. If you are to be persuasive, the more common ground you have – or appear to have – the more likely you are to persuade.

When we were producing advertisements targeted at women over 60 who wear size 20 dresses and bigger, do we find that the best ads are the ones with models who are over 60 and size 26? Of course not. Do the ads work best with a very young slim model? No. What works is a model we used to describe as being of 'indeterminate age – attractive but not beautiful'. Large, mature women found empathy with women who were how they *wanted* to be – how they *wanted* to see themselves – not how they actually were.

Bottled water. What's that all about? There are roughly 17 brands of bottled water in the average supermarket. Save the difference between still and sparking you can't tell the difference between one brand and another. Indeed, you would struggle to tell the difference between what my grandad called 'Corporation Pop' – the stuff that comes out of the tap – and any brand of water. Some labels make reference to the fact that this water has been in the mountains and fjords since time began and then they put a 'Use by November 2006' label on!

Why do people buy brands? Familiarity breeds acceptance and we buy what we are familiar with. Does Persil really wash whiter? Have you ever tested one shirt versus another with different detergents?

I thought not.

Welcome to empathy.

The lesson for you? Can you create greater empathy with the people you want to persuade? Undoubtedly so. 'Mirror' them and do what they do, be genuinely interested in their interests and, most importantly, tell them what you think they're good at. And don't buy an Ariel Arrow.

CHAPTER 18

Authority

We like to buy from people who know what they are doing, don't we? If I have a problem with my knee, I don't want to see a general practitioner – I want to see a knee specialist. We believe in specialists and what they say. If someone is positioned as an 'expert', what he or she says must be true, mustn't it?

I am a qualified football referee. I took up refereeing because all my sons play, and at junior football level it's not easy to get a referee. So I started refereeing, enjoyed it, and decided I would take the exams and qualify. Which then positioned me as an authority. I am now authorized to make the most awful decisions on a football field.

Linking this with 'rarity', the effect I have wouldn't work at the highest level of adult football because they *always* have a qualified referee. But at junior level, where it's often a 'track suit dad', I turn up with the full kit and the FA badge on my black referee's shirt. I check I have my yellow and red cards in full view of the players and allow them to see my preparation (two pencils, a coin and so on). The boys see the referee and often comment to each other, 'Proper ref this week'. The match is easier to referee because they see me as an authority – a qualified authority – and take my decisions much better than they would if I was not *perceived* to be a specialist, qualified individual.

Adrian Furnham is a friend of mine. Adrian is Professor of Psychology at University College London and is the second most productive psychologist in the world. I had occasion to introduce him at a conference in London and, in common with all speakers, he has a standard introduction. And as a fellow speaker I know the rules when introducing another speaker. You say what they want you to say. You don't ad lib or try a funny line because often the introduction itself is something the speaker works from.

So I was reading this intro and it said, 'Adrian Furnham is the second most productive psychologist in the world ...' And my subconscious was immediately doing what yours is probably doing now. Second! Who's first? I don't want to hear from number two – I want the best! Now, Adrian is an excellent speaker and quite possibly more entertaining and educational than the American who has written more papers and books; but we want *the* authority, don't we?

I'm sure people join the armed forces for a wide variety of reasons. Members of the emergency services and security guards very often have a great passion for the work they do and for many it is a true vocation. But a key aspect for some of these individuals is that they get to wear a uniform.

And that makes them an instant authority.

It means they command respect. Unless the uniform is that of a traffic warden, when the normal rules don't seem to apply. The bottom line is that we all see people differently when we see them as an authority and it's a key reason why we buy.

The lesson? Can you position yourself as more of an authority in the market that you're in? Can you qualify your product or service in some way? Have you won awards or been given formal recognition that positions you as the authority? If you can, it helps you to be persuasive.

CHAPTER 19

Special Deal

When I was at university I recall Professor Hammerton asking us to perform an experiment. He had three buckets of water. One contained extremely hot water – uncomfortably hot. One was at room tempera-ture and the third was extremely cold as it contained ice. The buckets were lined up together on a table with the lukewarm water bucket in the middle of the three. He had each of us put one hand in the hot water and one in the cold water and hold it there for a few seconds. Then he asked us to put both hands quickly in the lukewarm water. We then had to concentrate on what each hand felt like and describe it. Clearly, the warm water felt cold to the hand that had been in the hot water, and felt warm to the hand that had been in the ice-cold water.

Because the temperature we felt – relevant to what each hand experienced – was different. We mentioned the issue of expectation in Chapter 11, and your ability to persuade is, to a large extent, influenced in turn by what the persuadee's expectation is. Managing expectation is critical and in this chapter we examine that.

People don't want cheap brands but they do want brands cheap. Everybody wants a special price, a special 'deal'; and your ability to position your offer as a special deal is at the very fulcrum of the seven psychological reasons.

'Good cop/bad cop' works on this very principle. Let's summarize what 'good cop/bad cop' is about. Our 'accused' is in jail. 'Bad cop' reads the riot act to him. He tells him how bad the whole situation is. He even exaggerates how much evidence they have on the accused. If 'bad cop' has his way, our frightened individual will go down for a long time. No mirroring of body language, no sharing an experience. Just bad, bad news.

And then he leaves and 'good cop' enters the room.

He mirrors the individual's body language, he offers him a drink and they share that experience. He talks in a kinder tone and asks him to chat. He is a friend. Compared with the bad guy, this guy seems downright friendly. So he tells his story. It's become a special deal because relative to 'bad cop' this guy doesn't seem so bad at all. There are three key aspects to special deal:

- we all *want* to think we've done well;
- it's relative to something else; and
- it's not just about money.

A good salesperson can create empathy with a customer and then go along the lines of, 'I'll see if I can get my boss to agree to this'. The unseen boss is the 'bad cop' and the salesperson – the 'good cop'. It's a case of, 'Me and you, Mr Customer against the boss.'

My retail clients tell me it's so much easier to sell an expensive item first (for example a suit); *then* sell smaller, less expensive items such as a shirt and tie. The cost of a CD player or alloy wheels seemed relatively small once I had committed myself to nearly £10,000 worth of Volkswagen. Optional extras in kitchens usually put the price up appreciably, but once you have bought into that kitchen with that installer it's easier because, relative to the main cost, it doesn't seem a great deal. When there is a choice of three sizes (and costs associated with those sizes), inevitably the most popular size will be the middle one. The largest seems expensive and the cheapest seems small. And our beliefs and stereotypes come out here too. 'Expensive equals good.' (Remember our golf psychologist and my fear that if he's not very expensive he can't be very good?).

Do you remember the story of my wife and I in the furniture store to buy three sofas? The salesperson, a mature and extremely competent lady, had the 'tug' on the line. The final, discounted, price for the furniture was £4,678 and with me saying, 'Is that your best price?' she made a 'gesture' of £178.

It's 'only' 4% or so of the price and therefore she found it easy to give me this 'special deal'. Everything is relative in a 'special deal'. If someone made a 'gesture' of giving me £178 just for me asking him or her a question, I would be delighted. So when you are buying, use 'special deal' in this way. Remember that as the persuader is thinking big numbers you can get a better deal right at the end by asking for something that doesn't seem much, *relatively.*

Everyone selling anything has within their armoury a variety of components in the offer that has a higher perceived value to the customer or client than the actual costs to themselves. It could be free delivery, insurance/warranty, gift wrapping, time consultancy, quick turnaround, installation or whatever. Make sure you understand the value to your prospect and you can offer a great, special deal without too much cost to your self.

Some very good friends of ours have two daughters. The youngest one went to university in Exeter, which is a long drive from Harrogate. Anyway, after they had dropped her off at the Halls of Residence they didn't hear from her for quite a while. She must be the only 19-year-old I know without a mobile phone. Understandably, her mum and dad were really beginning to worry when, in November, they still hadn't heard from her. Indeed, our friends were going to drive down to Exeter for the weekend when they received this letter:

Dear Mum and Dad,

As you know, I've been at university for almost three months now and I would firstly like to apologize for not writing to you sooner. I am truly sorry for my thoughtlessness but things have been a bit hectic on campus to say the least.

Before I bring you up to speed with what's been happening it might be a good idea if you sit down. If you are already sitting down, you may even want to lie down. Either way, it is important that you do this before reading on. OK, I'll begin.

The good news is that, just like you said, the Fresher's Ball was an unforgettable experience and I got to meet a lot of new people. Paramedics, policemen and of course so many wonderful doctors who tell me that my skull fracture is now well on the way to healing. I don't actually remember jumping from my bedroom window, although when he visited me at hospital, the Chief Fire Officer did praise my presence of mind and said that he'd never seen a Halls of Residence go up quite so quickly – even with 30 little Christmas lights arranged so close to the curtains.

Fortunately, my fall was broken by Ben, the night watchman. He said I wasn't at all heavy in just my underwear and even carried me to his room in the Gate House to wait for the ambulance. Would you believe it took nearly an hour for them to arrive? Luckily Ben's a qualified First Aider and was able to give me the kiss of life and also massaged my heart several times to keep the blood circulating.

Anyway, until they rebuild the Halls, Ben has kindly invited me to share his flat with him. Some of the other girls have been a little horrid to me recently but I put this down to the shock of the fire and the fact that they're living in tents in the car park. Ben is a lot younger in outlook than he appears in real life and we've fallen deeply in love with each other and plan to marry. We haven't set a date yet, but it will have to be soon if I don't want to walk down the aisle with my bump showing.

Oh, yes, by the way, I'm pregnant. Isn't it marvellous news! I know how much both of you are looking forward to being grandparents because you talk about nothing else to my elder sister, Louise. Has she told you yet that she can't have children? It's so sad but, as they say, every cloud has a silver lining and I know you will welcome my baby and give it the love, devotion and tender care you gave to me when I was a child.

Now that I have brought you up to date, I want to tell you that there was no fire at the Halls, I did not fracture my skull, I am not engaged or even pregnant. There is no man in my life and as far as I know Louise can have children. However, I am getting a '3rd' in History and a 'fail' in Philosophy and I wanted you to see those marks in the proper perspective.

Your Loving Daughter,

Janie.

What a great way of using the 'Hot and Cold Contrast'! Compared with what they were *beginning* to think, a poor result is nothing at all.

'Buy one get one free' (often known as BOGOF) is the staple diet of all sales promotion. Buy product A and get product B free is also at the heart of many sales promotional ideas. The key for all marketing people is to have a high perceived value for product B but at a low real cost.

When we were working with Leeds United we came up with the idea of writing to season ticket holders asking them for details of their birthdays, family and of course, to recommend a friend. We were at the early stages of setting up a database so that we could write to people and sell Leeds United merchandise via the post. I explained to Bob Baldwin, the then marketing manager, that we needed some sort of incentive for people to respond and he suggested an out-of-date poster of the team.

The idea had many of the basic ingredients of sales promotion. It was a low real cost, because they'd already overprinted and had plenty in stock, but the high perceived value wasn't there. It was, after all, out of date. So I suggested that when we wrote to the supporters of Leeds United, the letter should come from the then manager, Howard Wilkinson. And the incentive to respond would be that Howard would ask them for their views on the team selection and tactics.

It seemed like a pretty good idea but I had no idea just how successful it would be. In my experience of direct mail it is by far and away the most successful percentage response I've ever experienced.

86% of season ticket holders wrote in with the information we required because it gave them the opportunity to tell Howard what they thought. We had people sending in bound documents, coloured illustrations, diagrams and wonderfully complicated hieroglyphics. All of which explained what Howard should do with his team and, of course, whom he needed to buy.

Boy was that an excellent incentive!

I'll leave it to you to decide how much attention Mr Wilkinson paid to the suggestions ...

When the BSE crisis became a big PR issue in Britain in the 1990s, I remember Chris Jacks at Asda telling me that in his experience, he had never seen such a marked decline in sales of a product than what happened to red meat. Overnight, people quite simply stopped buying it. But he said he also had never seen such a high dramatic increase in sales as when they reduced all red meat to half price. He said to me, 'Phil, I can only conclude that people are willing to die for half price!'

And why do retailers continue to price items at £9.99 rather than £10? Because it helps the feeling of 'special deal'. We're at the point where we want to buy and we're beginning to look for evidence to support our belief that this product is good value – that it's a good 'deal'. The fact that it's less than £10 or less than £100 helps to support our view that it's good value. There certainly can't be a *logical* explanation, can there?

But you have to be careful with 'special deal' and, as we said in negotiation, it needs to appear to be a struggle.

I worked in a large electrical retailers for the day. It was one of our advertising clients and I took the opportunity to don a white jacket and an 'I'm Philip and I'm here to help you' badge to see how people bought electrical appliances. The manager was keen to share his 20 years' plus experience with me and I listened with great interest as he told me his 'research' on how he developed the skill to sell television sets. It's perhaps important to point our here that in a typical electrical retailer, commission on sales forms a significant percentage of salary, so this was more than just academic interest in how and why people bought televisions.

He told me that his preferred technique was initially *not* to establish the individual's needs and budget, but, rather, to ask if the buyer (a high percentage of televisions are bought by males) would like to see the 'latest thing'? Invariably, the manager told me, men are interested in televisions and they would gladly follow his enthusiastic walk to the top of the range television. In case you haven't been to an electrical retailer recently, let me explain how it works. The televisions are typically stacked up against one wall with the highest priced TVs at one end and the cheapest at the other. They are typically graded by price rather than size, type and features.

So the manager leads the potential buyer to the most expensive television and explains all the features. He turns the features into benefits and the buyer becomes engaged. Only at this point does he appear to chastise himself for not asking about the customer's needs and says, 'I'm sorry I should have asked you; what sort of budget did you have in mind?'

Now, the top of the range television set can cost over £3000 but an average budget for someone coming into a store is £500. So our buyer explains to the manager that his budget is £500 and the manager says, 'I'm sorry. I should have taken you to those first. Let me show you the televisions at £500.'

So the manager guides the potential buyer down the line, but before he's arrived at the £500 televisions, the buyer is looking longingly over his shoulder at the most expensive television. This is a superb combination of the first impressions we talked about in Chapter 3 and also a great use of 'special deal'. The televisions at £500 seem rather disappointing compared with the new, top of the range product at over six times the price. The manager of the store explained to me that although it's rare for someone with a budget of £500 to spend over £3000, they invariably spend more to get some of the features they liked.

He then went on to explain that he'd carried out an 'experiment' for two weeks. 'It cost me a lot of money,' said the manager. For a fortnight, he told me, when someone said they were interested in televisions he took them to the bottom of the range. He explained that for around £99 you could have a good-quality colour television with remote control, 12 months' guarantee and with a reputable brand name. Again, he learned to almost chastise himself for appearing not to listen to the customer and then say, 'I'm sorry. I should have asked; what sort of budget did you have in mind for a television?'

On virtually every occasion, the manager told me, the prospective buyer would explain that he had a budget of £500 in mind but he was wondering if he needed to spend that much. He would be steered up to the £500 televisions but the chance of him spending more than £500 was almost non-existent. Indeed, on the vast majority of occasions he would spend *less* than £500 and hence the manager lost commission.

What a great way of using 'special deal'!

Everything's relative; it's the hot and cold contrast.

The Los Angeles-based Dr Kelton Rhoads has carried out research over a period of years in this area and the conclusion is very clear. In the absence of any other information, you will sell significantly more to a customer if you start at the most expensive product and work down rather than start at the bottom and attempt to work up. In many respects it cuts across so many views and beliefs I have about establishing the other person's needs first, and perhaps that's the point. Sometimes you can't establish the other person's needs. So the recommendation under those circumstances is always to start with your most expensive product. And, again, this ties in with negotiation. It's a lot easier to work down from a high price than it is to work up from a low one.

As a speaker, when I get a call from a new client asking if I can speak at their conference or convention the question they want to ask – but don't like to ask until later in the conversation – is, 'What is your fee?' Now the fee is always the same but the reaction to the investment varies enormously. If they are used to having speakers at their conferences it comes as no real surprise. If they don't have professional speakers they almost always are surprised at what they perceive to be a high cost.

Because everything is relative. From time to time an extremely high profile speaker enters the speakers' market. A John Major or Cherie Blair or, better still, a Bill Clinton or Colin Powell. They enter at a stratospheric fee level that raises the bar. And the rest of us can then increase our fees a little. It's the key to 'special deal'.

It's the psychology of 'special deal' that goes some way to explaining spoilt brats. Children brought up knowing they get what they want and being spoilt means they don't fully appreciate things when they come along. If you get used to always having your own way and pushing people around it becomes difficult for anybody to tell you differently. You can't play golf in Hanmer Springs *and* Banff *and* Gullane without the pain of air travel. No pain, no gain. Or, as we go on to say in Chapter 24, what goes up must come down. The tide goes in, the tide goes out. Yin and yang, zig and zag.

Welcome to 'special deal'.

And the lesson for you? Can you make it appear that right *now* is a great time to buy? Can you use the hot and cold contrast to make people 'feel' like they're getting a special deal? If you run a restaurant can you keep the prices where they are but have more expensive looking menus and better design? Create an aura of it being special so the prices are a pleasant surprise?

I was working with a group of CEOs not long ago and working through 'special deal'. I asked them to think whether there was an aspect of their service that had a high perceived value for the client but a low cost to them. Or consider whether they gave something away for free that a client would actually value. One MD told me that he always sent one of his well-qualified engineers out to do a survey of the client's needs whenever they were tendering for a big contract. It had a real value for the client (free consultancy, basically) but he was happy to do it because without the survey he would risk putting in a tender that didn't necessarily fully reflect the client's needs and it could cost them.

He decided to put a price on the 'survey' and have it available as a service. He called me a couple of months later and gave me the feedback. He had printed an A4 flyer that outlined in detail what was involved in the survey and costed it at £1500 + VAT. It was quite legitimately available for sale (and he would happily take business from it) but that wasn't the point. He had started using the flyer to explain to prospective clients what he was willing to do before they tendered and the client would see the cost. He said he actually enjoyed letting the client build up the belief that this was to be paid for before saying that, 'on this occasion' he was willing to do it for free.

Great example of 'special deal' at work and also he found the clients then felt obliged to him. Time for Chapter 20 and my second Biblical reference ...

CHAPTER 20

Obligation

In Galatians 6:7 it says, 'Be not deceived; God is not mocked: for whatsoever a man soweth, that shall he also reap.'

If you are invited to someone's house for a dinner party and you eat their food and drink their wine, do you feel obliged to have them back to your own home? Even if you don't like them? If you receive a Christmas card from someone who wasn't on your list, do you find a spare card and send them one back? If a friend says, 'Are you coming for a beer?' do you only have one beer or do you have two? If he buys the first beer, isn't it then your 'turn'?

Lindsey Chinar is someone I have known from birth. Her parents and my parents were very good friends and we saw a lot of each other. Indeed, her family were very good to me when I was growing up. When she married Andy Oultram, my wife and I saw Lindsey and Andy socially as we lived in the same area for a while. But they moved to Oxford and had three delightful children, and we moved to Yorkshire and, by coincidence, also had three of our own. And, as a consequence, we didn't see very much of each other but would keep in touch as best we could. When Lindsey heard I was changing careers she said to me, 'Anytime you're in Oxfordshire, Phil, you must come and stay'.

Which was nice.

An occasion came when I had to be in London one day and Cheltenham the next. So I called Lindsey and Andy and they very kindly invited me to dinner and stay overnight. I was more than happy to accept and we had a most delightful evening and they said, 'Any time, Phil. You must come again.' But despite the closeness of our relationship I feel rather guilty at going again until either Andy or Lindsey – or both of them – have come to stay at our home. I feel obliged.

She will, of course, be horrified that I feel this way but it's a natural psychological reaction, isn't it? It's what the hospitality industry relies on, after all. The seller wants the buyer to feel a little obliged.

Of course, there's plenty of logical justification about the ability to improve the relationship and discuss issues and there's nothing wrong with that. However, the deep psychological root is that people are building up obligations. Sellers are happy to build the buyer's conscience level.

I mentioned Bob Fern and his restaurant in Chapter 16. He told me that the percentage of people who simply didn't turn up after they had made a reservation was at a consistently higher level than he would like. I recommended he did two things. Firstly, ask them for their telephone number and also ask them if they would let him know if they had to change their plans.

And do you know what? People did.

The 'no show' percentage dropped dramatically as people either felt duty bound to turn up because they thought Bob might call, or they did call to tell Bob they had changed their plans. They had made a commitment and they then felt obliged.

Ever stopped at traffic lights and some guy jumps out and washes your windscreen even though you never asked? Find it hard not to open the window and pay something?

My wife goes to the extent of buying two or three small Christmas presents, wrapping them and keeping them to one side over the festive period just in case …

And how *not* to do it? My father was a professional buyer for a company called Paterson Zochonis. They're a Greek-owned company and, amongst other things, own Cussons. Hence their parent company name, PZ Cussons. Dad was a buyer for the chain of retail stores in West Africa and bought all manner of products. I recall just before Christmas each year he would hire a van to bring home all the products, gifts, bottles and give-aways he was given in the run up to Christmas. For me it was a real treasure trove and a day to look forward to.

I remember asking him who'd given him particular things and do you know what? He had no idea. He was given so much that it became ordinary, and there was no obligation because he couldn't even remember who had given him what. The point being, if you are going to work on obligation as a psychological reason, you have to make sure that what you do is memorable and highly relevant to the individual.

By far and away the most memorable (and commercially successful) hospitality I ever got involved in was running 'Father and Child Weekends'. I would invite clients and potential clients to bring their son or daughter, typically aged between 8 and 14, to spend a weekend in the Yorkshire Dales. We would climb, abseil, orienteer, canoe, pothole and generally have a challenging, educational and rewarding weekend. Even now, clients whose children are themselves married with children, tell me it remains one of the great highlights of their childhood.

But you can't *make* people feel obliged, can you? I also wouldn't suggest that you try and do it in some false way. If you are honest, sincere and genuine and want to be as helpful as you can towards your client, you'll find that he or she naturally becomes a little obliged to you. I always thought the most valuable information I could ever have about a particular client was his or her birthday.

I didn't need to know how old they were; just the day and month of their birthday. And I would send them a birthday card and small token on their birthday. I recall one client writing back to me and saying, 'In an ever-changing world it's a wonderfully reassuring thing to know that Phil Hesketh never forgets your birthday!' Did he feel obliged? I'll leave that to your own judgement.

Trust is the glue that holds relationships together, so everything must be done sincerely. But if you want to build a long-term relationship with your client, get him or her to feel a little indebted to you. Build their conscience level and give what you want to receive.

One of the most successful direct mail programmes I ran in the agency to help develop relationships with potential clients was what I called 'Playback'. In essence I offered a choice of three CDs (one pop, one classical and whatever was top of the album charts at the time) if they would reply on an easy-to-fill-in postcard and give me information that was pretty much easily available and public knowledge:

advertising spend, areas of interest, company size and so on. Importantly, when they received their free CD there was another card to fill in and another choice of three CDs. This time I wanted more detailed information, and typically over 80% who had responded to the first mailing replied again. And the third and final mailing was another choice of three CDs, a chance to win two tickets to a concert and, of course, I wanted even more information. Birthdays, personal interests, favourite sports and so on. Again, over 80% hung on in there.

I did it to gain information and allow me to move up the triangle of relationships, but what I also got was a feeling of indebtedness. Given the CDs were less than £30 for three and I only targeted companies who spent over £1m on advertising, it worked very well.

But to quote Samuel Butler, who wrote these words over 300 years ago: 'He that complies against his will, is of his own opinion still. Which he may adhere to, yet disown, for reasons to himself best known.'

Welcome to obligation.

And the lesson for you? Can you build up the conscience level with your client or customer so they feel a little indebted? Can you get your buyer to make a commitment to you so that he or she feels obliged? What can you give or say or do that would build up indebtedness?

If you own or run a ladies' dress shop and a lady is with her significant other, make a fuss of the guy. The older and wealthier he is, the bigger the fuss. Find him a seat; offer him a coffee and the day's newspaper. Make him feel important. Firstly, because he is; secondly, because you'll make him feel obliged; thirdly, because he'll have empathy with you and finally, because it might be me.

If you want someone to do something for you, ask him or her to write down their commitment and e-mail it to you. They'll feel much more obliged to carry out the action if they themselves have made the commitment.

Can you build those layers of tissue paper and do it with honesty, sincerity and a happy heart? Here are my five final thoughts on obligation.

- How do you get children to eat sprouts? Get them to grow them.
- Do what you say you're going to do.
- Remember that trust is the glue that holds relationships together.
- Everything must be done sincerely.
- Give what you want to receive.

CHAPTER 21

Nervousness

You know, coming up with acronyms takes ages. I don't mean the likes of BSE, USP and OTI. I mean the ones I've created, like BLUFF, FORM, NAIL, NEAT-NEAT and CRAWL. Acronyms that are created with the intention of helping people remember steps or a process. You probably think I knocked off the REASONS on a wet weekend in Yorkshire, but in truth it took me nearly twelve months. And when I say 'nervousness', what I really mean is *fear.*

Sometimes we buy things because we're frightened. Sometimes we buy because we're running away from the pain. It's a psychological fact that the fear of loss is a greater motivator that the desire to gain. And sometimes people will do things because they're frightened of what will happen if they don't. A remarkably high percentage of people buy a home security system within a few days of being burgled. They didn't have the need before, but now they're frightened.

Some people tell me they buy private education for their children because they're frightened of what the end product will be if they send them to the local state school. All we would need is the government of the country to say there's an extremely high risk of chemical warfare attack in Britain, and people would start buying gas masks, chemical suits and long-life torches. Petrol must be one of the few products that we all rush out and buy more of when the price goes up rather than down.

If there's a sugar shortage, people start stockpiling. A day or two before Christmas, panic sets in and all manner of festive products will sell because people are frightened. Even toilet rolls sell way above the average for the month. Old England Sherry becomes the brand leader for three weeks partly because people are frightened of what people will think if they call by and there's no sherry in the house.

Insurance companies, banks and building societies are going to great lengths to explain the ramifications of the low-growth forecast for low-cost endowment policies. Most holders of these policies are going to have a shortfall, but are putting their heads in the sand and doing nothing. It's only by using scare tactics they can get people to buy. Indeed, arguably all insurance is sold, to a greater or lesser extent, using this reason.

In advertising we found that selling a security alarm system for elderly people who lived on their own didn't work when we used the 'peace of mind' tactic. And the ad with the octogenarian sitting with her 55-year-old daughter, sharing a cup of tea and talking about how much comfort they had because the alarm system was in place, didn't work half as well as a photograph of the old dear on her own lying face down and in distress. Indeed, the ad improved as we closed in on the elderly lady's face and had her grimacing a little more. You have to be careful using fear as a motivator to sell, but the fact is, it is one of the seven REASONS spelled out at the end of Chapter 15.

Welcome to N-n-nervousness.

And the lesson for you? Well, of all the psychological reasons this is the one to be most careful to use. Is it the first time they're buying? What will happen if they don't buy *now*? Is it fair for you to point it out? Can you do it in a way that is persuasive? Fear can be a great motivator and persuades us to do many things we wouldn't do otherwise. But instil too much fear and you paralyze. Certainly, too much 'false fear' triggers stern resistance.

CHAPTER 22

Social Pressure

In Chapter 3 we talked about how to be more liked by more people, and the importance of doing what other people are doing. And that's the root of social pressure; we like to do what other people are doing.

I learned to play the guitar because I had a girlfriend when I was seventeen who could play very well and, indeed, performed in folk clubs in the area regularly.

She was called Stasia Cvenar.

Frankly, my burgeoning ego struggled with people buying me free drinks simply because I was attached to her and I resolved to play the guitar myself.

I went out the morning after one particularly embarrassing session whilst she was playing and bought Bert Weedon's *Play With Yourself in a Day* (or at least that's what I think it was called) and taught myself 'The Boxer' by Paul Simon. It was pretty soon after that I latched on to Ralph McTell's music and it became a burning passion. I still have the holes in my pockets to prove it.

I had a regular spot in The Broadoak Hotel in Ashton under Lyne playing three or four numbers in the interval every other Wednesday when a quite well-known band called The Fivepenny Piece was playing.

Flushed with my moderate success and not, at that early stage, realizing that I was never good enough to make it, I started busking. What I'd failed to spot was that other buskers always put coins in their cap or guitar case before they even started to play. It was sometime before I realized that people don't put money in an *empty* cap.

They need to see that other people have also put money in. We like to do what other people are doing. In the1970s, supermarkets briefly stocked tins of Heinz Baked Beans in an impressive pyramid shape that caught the shopper's eye. The trouble was, no one wanted to be first to take a tin and spoil the effect. Learning their lesson, supermarkets now leave one or two gaps on the shelves when stocking product to encourage people to take one. And have you noticed how press ads and TV commercials use expressions such as 'Everybody's buying'? It explains why you never see a successful busker with no money in his cap.

You like to do what everybody else is doing.

Do you want to sit in an empty restaurant or one that's really popular? That's the reason why waiters fill the window tables first. It looks popular and attracts people in. Personally, I want to have lunch in The Ivy. Everybody tells me, 'everybody goes there' so I want to go. I don't care what the food's like, nor the service. They could serve me a lettuce leaf in a dog bowl and I'd be happy. I just want to do what everybody else is doing.

It's always interesting to stand in a lift and observe people's body language change.

Everyone stares at the numbers on the lift and we act and behave in the way that people act and behave when they are in a lift. We do what everybody else is doing.

I was approached by a lady selling for Barnardo's recently. We got chatting because she was on the high street with her brochures and forms to sign people up. I noticed that there were three other representatives on the same street and I asked her if it was a particular technique or tactic. She told me that it wasn't something that they had been advised to do but she said that she had much more chance of getting someone to sign up to a standing order when they can see that *someone else* is also signing up.

We like to do what other people are doing.

It's how testimonials work. Testimonials work best when the prospective customer can see that a client in their industry (who is like them) has also found the person to be satisfactory. On a personal level, TDG Logistics were interested in me because of the work I'd done for

Exel Logistics. One big accountancy firm wanted to use me because they saw two of their competitors using me. FMCG clients want to see testimonials from other FMCG clients and so on.

My wife is an English teacher. She has taught for many years at what she describes as 'a nice school with nice children with nice, caring parents'. Whilst she has the highest possible opinion of the school and its staff, she wanted to work in a poorly performing school in a deprived area. And that could be easily arranged!

What she found in terms of disciplining these badly behaved children from underprivileged areas was that she had to get the 'chief whinge' on her side. It was not enough for her to talk to the students and get them to behave in a better way and be more interested in the subject. She had to get the ringleaders to be on side. Because people do what other people are doing. Or, at least, they do what their peers and the people they respect are doing. So often, she would tell me, the students with real potential would develop bad habits and fall in with a bad crowd because of what she described as 'peer pressure'. As mentioned in Chapter 15, Professor David McLelland spent a lifetime (mainly at Harvard) concluding that the biggest single factor in stopping people being successful when it seemed like all the ingredients were there, was hanging out with the wrong crowd. I adopted and adapted my wife's expression, 'peer pressure' and called this psychological reason 'social pressure'.

The lesson for you?

Can you use testimonials? Can you use the fact that other people buy your product? Can you encourage people to buy because other people – just like them – are buying? If you are looking for charity sponsors because you are running a marathon or being silent for 24 hours – or whatever – make sure the first three or four people put down big amounts. Ask the people with money first and after that people will feel they 'should' sponsor you for £10 (if that's what the first sponsors did) rather than 50p.

CHAPTER 23

Putting the Reasons Together

So, Ralph McTell. What's all that about?

I mentioned in Chapter 1 that I want to play live with Ralph McTell. Why? I don't really know. And when we come to look at motivation in Chapter 26, you'll see that my personal view is that you don't need to know *why* you want to do a certain thing. The key is whether you know what it is and whether you have the emotional desire to do it. So how can I use the psychological reasons to get Ralph McTell to want to play live with me? What *form* will his motivation take? Fun? Obligation? Running Away? Money?

Well, on every professional speaking engagement I have, I make reference to Ralph McTell. I have, as a prop, a guitar that I never play. I play his CDs at courses, conventions, conferences, seminars and workshops all around the world and the intention is that I shall introduce Ralph McTell to a whole new audience. Basically, I am Ralph McTell's one-man marketing machine. For free.

Why am I doing this? Because Ralph McTell will get to hear about me if, as planned, I become the best speaker on the planet. And then one day we'll meet. He'll make reference to the fact that it's a very rare thing for someone to go to such trouble (Rarity). He'll tell me that he likes me doing what I do and, therefore, that he likes me (Empathy).

I'll be able to tell him I'm the authority on Ralph McTell music and can talk about the 17 albums I have of his (Authority). He'll recognize that this is a great deal for him and may even offer to refund my money. Just a thought. He'll realize that I'm doing all this promoting and hopefully making him more money and giving him a bigger audience and there's no charge (Special Deal). And, importantly, he'll tell me he feels obliged (Obligation). He'll ask me how he can ever repay me.

I shall say that there is one thing he can do for me. He can appear live with my son Daniel and I at the Royal Albert Hall. And we can play 'Nanna's Song'.

Well, at least I've got a plan.

On our first night in Auckland just before I started to write this book, my wife and I went to a restaurant by the harbour called Cin Cin's. It was 7 p.m. so we thought we would be able to get a table reasonably easily. What we didn't appreciate was that New Zealanders tend to eat a little earlier than we do in Britain, and the maitre d' came over and asked if we had a reservation. I explained that we didn't and could we have a table for two? He grimaced a little and said he would see what he could do.

I thought, 'This is excellent'.

He's already using 'rarity' (difficult to get a table) and 'social pressure' (everybody eats here) and he came back and said he could 'squeeze us in'.

Get in!

He's using 'special deal' as well. Would we like to have a drink at the bar whilst they sorted the table for us?

So as we approached the bar I asked my wife, as I have done for 30 years now, what she would like to drink. And, as she has done since we met in the 1970s, she couldn't make up her mind. Eventually she settled on the same choice she's had for over 30 years and I was about to order, when the maitre d' said our table was ready. I said could we just have a drink at the bar but he was keen to get us to the table. What a waste!

He then asked if we wanted water, but by that stage our mouths were salivating for alcohol, thanks very much, and could we have a drink? Do you know what he did? He said, 'Let me get you some water first.' What a lost opportunity! In the end we had a delightful meal but he missed out on the sale of an extra couple of drinks, and instantly ruined the obligation he'd built up by being what *he* thought was helpful but which left us feeling like just another couple of punters.

This is going on all the time.

One of the pharmaceutical companies I work with sells products to farmers and vets. And in the past, they've had marketing people from head office making presentations on new drugs to these people.

Wrong.

When we asked ourselves the question, 'Who does the farmer have greater empathy with, a vet or a drugs company executive, suited and booted?', the answer was clear. When we asked, 'Who is the authority for the farmer? A vet, another farmer who has used the product, or the city slicker from head office?', again it is a straightforward answer. So now they do things differently. Instead of the suited marketing man, they get working vets who have used the new drug to make the presentation. Ideally, they also have a farmer present who also has experience of the drug and found it to be easy to use, effective and good value.

Car sales people use 'special deal' (relative price) by not adding on the extras such as CD players and so on until you're committed to the main price. My wife spent more than £300 on designer clothes recently and I felt no guilt in buying an item for £50 whilst she continued to browse. *Relatively* it wasn't a lot. Fashion is interesting because most fashion items move from 'rarity' when a new fashion comes in, to 'social pressure' as a style becomes popular, to 'special deal' when it's put on sale because it's gone the way of the shell suit. What goes around comes around.

Most times on aeroplanes I sit in economy class. Occasionally the client pays for me to go business class, but mainly I'm on the wrong side of the curtains. Selling that premium service effectively uses a combination of 'rarity', 'ego' and 'social pressure.' Firstly, there are fewer business class seats than there are economy. It takes a certain ego to want to travel and pay that level of premium but you want to be the sort of person who's seen to be the sort of person who travels in business class. You pay quite a premium, and people upgrade and pay more because of an emotional desire. They then justify the decision with logic but they have already made the decision.

People have to make up their own mind on whether the premium is worth it. Personally, I can produce a long list of other things I'd rather do with the £3000 it costs to upgrade my wife and I to fly business class to New Zealand. But I do understand why people want to do it. There's something about the curtains, isn't there? It's separating the Joneses from the hoi polloi that makes the difference. What I don't understand is why business class isn't at the back of the plane rather than the front. Surely it's safer there. After all, you never hear of a plane *reversing* into a mountain, do you?

And I never understood the Post Office's distinction between first and second class stamps. Are the second class stamps put at the back of the train with curtains between them and the first class stamps so that they can't see the fun those privileged envelopes are having? Answers on a postcard.

Whatever you sell, it isn't a case of 'choosing' which one of the psychological reasons you can best employ. You almost certainly use several. The key is to recognize that, to explore what you can develop and, perhaps establish one of the *reasons* you are not exploiting as much as you might.

And the seven psychological REASONS offer us help with life itself. The 'S' of 'Special Deal' in the middle tells us that everything is relative. We in Britain appreciate the sunshine in summer because our autumns and winters are cold, dark and too long. Well, they are in Ashton. A hot bath and clean bed linen are such delights when you have been camping in a hot, sticky climate. But then it becomes ordinary. Remember the bacon sandwiches?

The 'S' in the middle (see Figure 23.1) is also the fulcrum of a see-saw. Life has its ups and downs, and the highs are only appreciated by the fact there *are* lows. And at one end of the see-saw we have 'Rarity'.

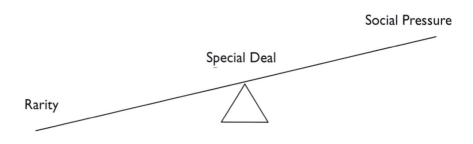

Figure 23.1 *REASONS see-saw*

We all need special treats. We all need some surprises and, by definition, some uncertainty.

At the other end of the see-saw there is 'Social Pressure.' We all need to belong. We want to feel comfortable. We need certainty in out lives. We need to feel that what we are doing is normal. There is a rhythm to winter, spring, summer and autumn. A rhythm to the passing of the months that make the year, as Ralph McTell puts it.

PART 6

Business, Motivation and Doing Something About It

CHAPTER 24

The Five Things that Matter in Business

It could be argued that there are only *three* things that matter in business: finding customers, keeping customers happy so they stay with you and, of course, making money. The fundamentals of business boil down to those *three* things, right? You have to get customers or clients in the first place, you have to deliver and do what you say you're going to do and offer a good service (or your clients and customers don't come back), and you need to make sure all the systems and the margins are in place to make money.

But there's more to it than that, isn't there? I believe that there are two other factors: constantly being aware of change and motivating your *own* people and colleagues.

Let me tell you about the 'Serenity Prayer'. The original version was written on a piece of paper by Reinhold Niebuhr as his closing prayer in a church service. Afterwards, upon request, he gave it to a friend and it became famous when it was used for his obituary in the local newspaper. Amongst others, the AA (think alcohol breakdown, not roadside assistance) use the 'Serenity Prayer' and it has brought help to many recovering people as they attempt to accept a disease, take stock of their situation and move forward and make amends. This is how it goes:

> 'Give me the serenity to accept the things I cannot change, the strength to change the things I can and the wisdom to know the difference.'

The point is, we live in a world of constant change. Indeed, it's the only thing that's constant. And persuasion techniques change, too.

I don't have any client who wants to sound like a salesman. I don't know anyone who goes onto an exhibition stand or into a shop or company's office, and enjoys the 'feeling' that the vultures are swooping; that the sellers can smell fresh meat. I don't know anyone who sees the salesperson's rictus smile and doesn't recoil. I don't know anyone who enjoys the salesperson 'taking control'. I don't know anyone who says, 'Look what someone sold me today.'

Unless it's negative.

But there are still some dinosaurs. There are still some Neanderthal clubbing men and women out there.

So if you are wondering how the 'foot-in-the-door' salesman does establish control and you want to stop it, here is some advice.

Firstly, there are various ploys these unscrupulous people have. When they arrive on the doorstep they often do so without a presenter or briefcase, unannounced and probably 15–20 minutes before an appointment was due, and begin with an apology along the lines of, 'Sorry our salesman could not come. I'm a director of the company, can I just have a quick chat with you?' They establish a false authority and often the unsuspecting homeowner will let them in straight away.

Typically no one will keep a 'director' on the doorstep.

As the 'director' – you appreciate this is actually just the salesman who is calling – has walked in unannounced, the radio or TV might be on so the first thing they do is to switch it off and sit down. Then they invite the householders to do the same.

And in switching off the TV, they're doing what?

They're establishing total control here. They have gone into someone's house, into their space and taken charge. They haven't asked permission to switch off the TV because it's a distraction – they've just done it. They've also sat down before the home owner has said, 'Please sit down.'

Their aim of establishing control is to then bring the homeowners into the area where they might sign something. As a reader you are probably thinking, 'I'd throw someone out if they came into my home and did that.' And I'm sure you would. Indeed, you should. But for the unscrupulous salesperson, either result is a good one. If he or she is thrown out, it has saved them a lot of time. Because the ones that haven't thrown them out are those that they know they can control.

Step two is, they look for family photos and create false empathy. Often step three is that they use the 'I'll make you famous' or, 'We just happen to be in your street today' techniques.

For example, the salesman might begin with, 'Could we use your house in a brochure? We want to use it to show our new windows?' and go on to say, 'We can only do this price today so you've got to decide today.'

It's horrocks. Call the Office of Fair Trading.

Unfortunately they are using many of the psychological REASONS and older people, in particular, need to be warned against them. Don't feel obliged, don't let empathy get in the way of logic, don't believe the 'deal' is only available today and don't be led down the path of thinking that lots of people are buying right now.

I went on a bit of a rant there for three reasons.

- Vulnerable people should be made aware of unscrupulous people and the Office of Fair Trading can help enormously.
- This is such an old-fashioned way of selling. It is interesting that it is predominantly now only used with older people. It doesn't work on most people because they see the techniques and the lack of genuine care.
- It illustrates the need for buyers to know more about selling and persuading.

I want you to imagine that you are learning to play tennis for the very first time. And I want you to imagine two scenarios. The first scenario is that you find that you are innately good at tennis and that you have a gift for the game. With regular lessons and practice you are getting better by the day. You are enjoying the game and enjoying your improvement. Friends of yours who also decided to pick up the game at the same stage are not so gifted.

So whilst playing them in the first week or two was quite enjoyable because you were at the same standard, it's now becoming quite easy to beat them. But, in this first scenario, I want you to imagine that you're only allowed to play people at that poor standard despite the fact that your own game is getting better. How does that feel? It's frustrating, isn't it? When your skills improve but the challenge doesn't, you become bored and you question whether it's worthwhile to continue with the game, as it's become too easy.

In the second scenario I want you to imagine that you have started to play tennis but find that you have no particular gift. You like the game and are having lessons but to no avail. Let's not put too fine a point on this – you are not 'The Chosen One'. You miss the ball often and that's just when you're trying to serve. But in this scenario the tennis club that you're a member of insists you play against people of a good standard. Your friends all around you are improving rapidly and each time you go on to the court you know you're going to lose. Indeed, you're not too far from humiliation each time. Now how does that feel? It's frustrating, isn't it?

You're entering the triangle of anxiety in Figure 24.1 and, again, you question whether or not you want to continue to play because there is little or no pleasure.

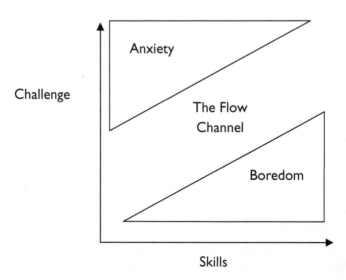

Figure 24.1 *Triangles of anxiety and boredom*

The triangles of anxiety and boredom exist in life itself. The secret, of course, is to be in what is described in the diagram as 'The Flow Channel'. This is how movies are made. Look at the big blockbuster movies of our time and observe how the writer, director and producer structure the story so that you become anxious and worried about our hero or heroine. Will Kate Winslet and Leonardo DiCaprio make it off the *Titanic* alive? Will Bruce Willis be able to undo the handcuffs in the burning building? How will James Bond get out of such a tight spot?

We don't want to watch a film that takes us into the triangle of boredom. We need a film that grips us, that makes it interesting by taking us into the triangle of anxiety and then back into 'The Flow Channel.' It's the same principle as the psychological reason 'special deal'. Films that end with the 'happy ever after'-type scenario leave us right back there in 'The Flow Channel', whereas tragedies such as *Romeo and Juliet* leave us sanguine and reflective as we walk out of the theatre. *Fahrenheit 9/11* deliberately leaves us in the anxiety triangle. Or at least that's where Michael Moore wanted you to be.

Comedies ensure that our hero keeps making the same mistake. Laurel and Hardy got this off to a fine art. It explains the attraction of watching great sporting events and explains why football rather than rugby, cricket and golf is our biggest spectator sport. Because, in the FA Premier League, any one team can beat another during any match throughout a season. We actually enjoy the roller-coaster ride of being taken into the anxiety triangle. Of course, we complain bitterly as we sit in the stands when our team is losing, but if our team won every single game easily we would simply enter the triangle of boredom.

By far and away my best sporting moment as a spectator was when my eldest son and I went to Barcelona on 24 May 1999 to watch Manchester United play Bayern Munich in the European Champions League Final. My eldest son had his 18th birthday just a few days before and my present to him was a ticket to see the final. (I had been at Wembley in 1968 when United beat Benfica 4–1 and was probably one of only a few thousand in the stadium that night who had been to both finals.) With ninety minutes gone in the game and the fourth official showing that there were only three minutes of injury time left, my subconscious mind was well into the triangle of anxiety and my conscious mind was preparing for the worst – and firmly rooted in the triangle of boredom. When Manchester United scored two goals in the final three minutes to win the game – and my son and I were behind the goal at El Camp Nou – we shared a very special experience. But if Manchester United had scored two goals early on, the thrill wouldn't have been the same.

People often ask me, 'Why should I step outside of my comfort zone?' and the answer is, 'You don't have to.' But you run a severe risk of festering in the triangle of boredom for the rest of your life if you don't experience anxiety at some point.

In the same way that there are only a certain number of types of films that have ever been made, there are similarly, in my view, only six 'types' of songs that have ever been written.

- 'I love you' songs. Expressing your undying love for someone by definition takes you into the anxiety triangle, as you're wanting reciprocation.
- 'I'm leaving you/have left you and am coming back because I love you.' Anxiety created by whether or not you'll be there when I come back and you'll still love me etc.
- 'You're leaving me/have left me but you'll be coming back.' Again, the anxiety and tension created, *à la*, 'Will you still love me tomorrow?'
- 'I'm leaving you and I'm glad to be gone.' Anxiety created by leaving and if you don't find another love you'll go into the triangle of boredom.
- 'You're leaving me and thank God you've gone.' Enough said; 'I've had enough pain and anxiety.'
- Protest and novelty songs. Bob Dylan made a career out of these, and whoever wrote a protest song without in someway feeling angry, anxious and tense? There are of course, some novelty songs that don't really fit into these categories that I never really quite got. 'Ernie (The Fastest Milkman in the West)' driving a really fast milk cart. And 'Puff the Magic Dragon' apparently lived by the sea, but beyond that I'm at a loss to understand what either was about.

So without entering the triangle of anxiety or leaving your comfort zone, how do you achieve anything? How will you ever be more persuasive if you don't start using these techniques?

Today.

All frustration is due to unfulfilled desires, and I hope that in reading this book you will see your way to achieving more, because you will become more persuasive and influential. In addition to the reasons why people buy products, services and excuses, we also have certain needs. Of course, as we discussed in Chapter 14, we have a need for food, shelter, warmth and so on. But one of the ironies of life is that we have a need for certainty *and* uncertainty. If everything is certain we enter the triangle of boredom, but if everything is uncertain we spend our whole life being anxious.

I am sitting in Heathrow Airport at 8.30 p.m. My flight to Leeds/Bradford is scheduled to leave at 9 p.m. but there is bad weather. The authorities *know* where the plane is, so why don't they tell us? If the voice on the Tannoy tells me that the plane is on the ground and that the wait is just for one hour, I can quickly come to terms with it, buy a drink and a magazine and plan what I will do with the hour.

Frustration and anxiety are creeping in as I'm being told either nothing at all or simply that there's a delay. People around me are shifting uneasily in their seats. Will they get home tonight? How long is the delay? Do they need a hotel room? What are the ramifications for tomorrow's board meeting, a son's sports day or a wedding anniversary?

We all have lives to live.

The less you know, the more anxious you become, and it's a constant frustration for me and many other air travellers that airlines and airports don't truly care about their customers. If they did they would tell us what was happening all the time. Give us the truth; tell us exactly where we stand and tell us right away.

The plane has been on the ground all the time. The plane is to be just 40 minutes delayed. Why not tell us?

You need pain to change and everything starts with desire. It's a fact of life that both good and bad things will happen to you along the way. Many of the bad things will be beyond your control, so why worry about them? And when the good things happen, don't forget to enjoy them and celebrate every precious moment. But in addition to this, there's also 'inevitable' change.

Some years ago, I read *The Decline and Fall of the Roman Empire* by Edward Gibbon. It's almost as tough as Stephen Hawking's *A Brief History of Time*, but appreciably longer. To save you reading it, let me tell you what happens.

The Romans were ambitious. They grew and grew their empire and, as my mother would say, 'went conquering'. Over the years the upper classes became incredibly idle. They had spread well away from their roots in Italy and there were no mobile phones, laptops and e-mail back then to stay in touch. So people stopped communicating, particularly at the edges of the empire. Hubris and disunity settled in. They became complacent and arrogant, and at the very heart of the empire in Rome, children didn't want to be anything else but soldiers. The poor had enough bread, cheap meat and wine to eat and drink, as well as chariot races to watch. But eventually there was no fresh supply of slaves from subject races. Its far-flung borders had become hard to control and the Emperor Constantine in AD 330 established a fine new capital in Byzantium. He even had the arrogance to rename it Constantinople.

Top prize for arrogance, however, must go to Julius Caesar for pinching the Egyptian calendar and renaming it the 'Julian Calendar'. So that it all fitted neatly together, he lengthened the year of its introduction to 445 days, which caused a bit of disquiet amongst some of his subjects who were a bit peeved that he hadn't thrown in a few more Bank Holidays to compensate. However, he didn't stop there. In his honour, he decided to rename the seventh month July. Later, not to be outdone, his successor, Augustus, renamed the eighth month after himself.

And when did they start using the terms BC and AD? Who decided one day that henceforth we would use this particular system? Obviously not before AD 0. Well, the calendar we use is known as the

Gregorian calendar, as it was Pope Gregory who tidied it all up towards the end of the 16th century. But history suggests it was a Russian monk, Dionysius Exiguus, who was asked by the Pope at the time – John I – to sort out the dates for Easter. Dionysius decided to start with when Jesus was born. It was he, apparently, who plumped for December 25 – thereby putting Christmas on the map. (It was a Roman civic holiday anyway.) So our calendar was worked out in 527 by a Russian sitting in Italy based on stories that were written over the previous six or seven hundred years.

Fascinating. Back to the story of the Roman Empire.

In AD 410 it was pretty much all over when Honorius became leader. Unlike his macho predecessors, he wasn't at all keen on that military 'thing', and much preferred poultry farming instead. So when the Visigoth troops came knocking on his door, it was pretty much game over. Or poultry over, if you prefer. After all, there's not much you can do against a savage army when your defence is made up largely of battery hens. Feed them, and hope they go away, perhaps.

I am not making this up.

Recently I read *The Rise and Fall of Marks & Spencer* by Judi Bevan. Do you know what? It's the same story. For Honorius in 410 read Rick Greenbury in 1998. They stopped listening to their customers, they became arrogant and complacent and didn't respond to inevitable change. Like Honorius, M&S had become introspective and obsessed with their own product and had not looked at the change around them. The only difference between the two was their standard of underwear. Arguably, Margaret Thatcher was in the same mould – a leader who didn't recognize the time to go. History is full of stories of people who just didn't see it coming. Caesar didn't know Brutus was not on his side until the last minute. And what was the man who chopped down the last tree on Easter Island thinking about?

I've read the biographies of both John Lennon and Paul McCartney about the rise and fall of The Beatles. It took appreciably less time than the Roman Empire and Marks & Spencer but the story is largely the same. It's one of ambition, growth, desire and teamwork. Then as success takes hold of people's senses, this changes to arrogance and complacency and the setting in of hubris. Poor old George couldn't get his work onto the albums because Lennon and McCartney were hog-ging the limelight, and they had in-fighting just as the Romans before them and the M&S after them.

If you compare these stories with the collapses of the Mayan civilization at the end of the ninth century, the Anasazi Indians in the late 1200s, Easter Island in the 17th century and much more recently the Soviet Union, the common thread is that the steep decline tends to follow very swiftly after the peaks. And that's why there is more to business than just getting customers, keeping customers happy and making money.

The fourth thing that matters in business is that *you have to be con-stantly aware of change and motivating your own people.*

For a fine example of change and its inevitability, it's useful to look at the holiday market. In the early 1970s, holidaying abroad was for a very small percentage of people. Indeed, only a handful of Britons held passports. Then, as package tours arrived in the mid- to late '70s, we all clambered for the package tour holiday to Spain. Benidorm and Tor-remolinos replaced Blackpool and Torquay and good old fish and chips was substituted by plates of paella. And chips, if you really must.

But, as I write, sales of holidays to Spain are at an all-time low, with some mass-market operators still holding 40% of unsold holidays, despite a third successive summer of discounts in the peak period of July and August.

Of course, it would be easy to blame the war in Iraq, the weather or the football, but that would be dodging the real issue of inevitable change. Two major things have happened to create that change. Firstly, our skill level – or in this case, our desire for adventure – has expanded to such an extent that for many of us, simply going to Spain is no longer exciting. To spend two weeks lying on a slab on the Costa del Sol is, for many, entering the triangle of boredom. Not to be confused with the Bermuda Triangle, which is a good way further west.

And the other key factor, of course, is the Internet. These days you don't need to go to a travel agent to book a holiday – you can book online, you can fix up car hire and insurance, and you can pick and choose how long you go for and in what hotels. Add to that the huge growth in low-cost flights available on the web and the acceleration of change is there to see. Ticket-only sales with airlines and accommo-dation-only sales are up, whilst sale of package tours are down. New Zealand, Australia and Taiwan are no longer regarded as long-haul holidays for the discerning and mature traveller.

We live on planet holiday.

Will the package holiday return? In its current format? Will we go back to Torremolinos and Benidorm in the numbers we used to? Will the Italians run Europe again? Would The Beatles have ever reformed, even when it was possible? Will Marks & Spencer become great again? The answer to the final question is, possibly, if they rediscover what the market wants and change themselves.

And that's the real challenge facing all businesses. That's the fifth 'thing' that matters in business; *the desire to seek new ways of doing things*. Persuasive techniques have changed and the classic 'hard sell' that I was introduced to in the 1970s – and, indeed, was a reasonable exponent of – is laughed at by people who have wised up on selling techniques. We need to be persuasive in a very different kind of way. We need to be persuasive by finding out what it is that the other person needs. And that's not just about their logical, stated needs, it's about their psychological needs. It's about understanding what the other person really wants out of it all.

It's about not looking and sounding like a vulture that has spotted his breakfast.

Summary? Accept that change is inevitable and anticipate it. People who make money out of stocks and shares tell me that the secret is to sell *before* the market gets to the top. What goes up must come down. The tide goes in, the tide goes out. Yin and yang, zig and zag. If you are not part of the steamroller, you're part of the road.

CHAPTER 25

The Seven Great Myths of Life

I am sitting in Djerba in Tunisia. This morning I spoke for three hours at a conference and now I'm relaxing on the beach. This is a perfect day: the sun is hot and the beer is cold. Better still, the beer, food and fluffy beach towel are all provided by the hotel, all of which are paid for by the client.

Excellent.

Except that I am not with the people I love. To be enjoyed, experiences have to be shared. The idea that if you escape from the monotony and drudgery of everyday life and are able to lie on a beach, that you will then be happy, is one of the great myths of life. Because if you do escape from the daily grind, you also escape from the challenge. And where will you be after a day or two? You lose the 'rarity' – it's no longer special. You enter the triangle of boredom.

It's the first great myth of life. That everything will be all right when you sell up and can lie on a beach. That happiness will be achieved when the next thing happens or, worse still, when you 'get' the next 'thing'. Happiness is the journey, not the destination. And it's all connected to 'rarity'. We seek the things we can't have thinking that they will give us joy. And they do. Until they become 'everyday' and treated as 'givens'.

The second great myth of life is 'I want, doesn't get'.

It's horrocks.

If you have children you'll know that they can be extremely persuasive. They keep asking you for that ice cream or that day trip. They persist and nag and keep at it. And, as a result, they often get what they want.

Being persuasive is often about dogged tenacity. Many clients of mine have become so after years and years of mailing, calling and generally keeping in touch with them. I prefer the Geordies' expression; 'Shy bairns get nowt'.

The third great myth of life is, 'You can screw people without consequence'. I have preached honesty as the single most important factor for persuading and I repeat that plea now. I made my second Biblical reference in Chapter 20 that you 'reap what you sow' and let me make my third and final reference to the Bible now.

In Ecclesiastes 11:1 it says, 'Cast thy bread upon the waters; for thou shalt find it after many days.' My grandad used to say, 'Cast thy bread upon the waters and it will come back to thee pobs'. To explain, my grandad had a cynical sense of humour and 'pobs' is a Lancastrian word for wet toast. My grandma used to say to him, 'Have patience. Job had patience.' And my grandad used to say 'Yes, but Job didn't have my bloody corns.'

In today's business relationships you can't run the risk of cheating and ripping people off for very long. Not only will you get found out and the law of causality will kick in, but you have to live with yourself too. The law of causality states that for every action there is an equal and opposite reaction, and I believe that to be the case. Deal with everyone honestly, tell the truth and you'll find in the long term, you'll be well respected and therefore more persuasive.

Remember that if you never tell a lie you don't have to remember anything.

Myth number four is that you *should* always do what your mother says. People are often told what they *should* do based on pre-conceived ideas and beliefs of what will happen. But they're just beliefs and, as we said in Chapter 1, most beliefs aren't true. If you're not careful, people will *'should'* all over you – so don't always do what you *should* do.

Are you familiar with the expression, 'If you always do what you've always done, you'll always get what you've always got'? That's myth number five. Its origin is lost in the mists of time and it is often used to make the point that you need to create change. But I think it's horrocks. As we saw in Chapter 24 everything is either growing or in decline. If you keep doing what you've always done you won't get the same result, you will actually get *less*. Because the world is changing all around us and you need to keep up with change just to stand still.

I'm sure you have heard, 'If it ain't broke, don't fix it'.

It is myth number six.

So what about your car, your house, indeed your body? They may not be broken but they decay and problems occur unless you carry out proper maintenance. So this is horrocks too. You need to nurture all your client relationships and ensure that you are constantly looking to improve. You need to hone your persuasive skills and expressions all the time.

A friend of mine came to me in tears one day. 'My wife's left me,' he said. 'I haven't done anything.'

Nothing more needs to be said.

In New Zealand there is a mythical dragon called the Taniwha. It's not quite the antipodean equivalent of the Bogey Man – the belief is that the Taniwha *wants* to live in harmony with man, whereas the Bogey Man just wants to get you. If you disturb the Taniwha in some way it comes to get you. People say that there is a Taniwha in a particular location where the plan is to build a motorway. It's used as a deterrent to the authorities – a false threat that they will suffer if the route is built – and the people who use the motorway will have accidents. People all over the world create their own Taniwhas. The myths are perpetuated and people finish up believing that things aren't possible. Ironically, the seventh myth originates in a country that for many people couldn't possibly have existed because they believed that the earth was, after all, flat.

Myths abound. It's time to talk about motivation and the steps to success.

CHAPTER 26

Motivation and the Six Steps to Success

In Chapter 1 I explained that I began to write this book on February 25, 2004. My motivation came from wanting to be the best speaker on the planet and to aid and abet that desire I needed to write a best-selling book. To motivate myself to ensure the book was finished, I needed to know where it would be launched and, indeed, needed to 'picture' the book in a bookstore.

I recall reading Bob Rotella's book on golf psychology. In it he wrote, 'I was approached by Seve Ballesteros at the Winchester Classic. He said "Nick Price says I need to talk to you. He says you'll teach me how to win again. He said what you teach is the future of golf. Once," Seve went on glumly, "I was the future of golf. All I ever did for years is what I think you teach. I just saw myself in my mind winning golf tournaments. I saw myself making the shots. I saw myself winning. The year I won the US Masters by seven or eight shots I knew that I would win it before the plane landed in America. The only problem was that as I walked up the eighteenth fairway I did so without any joy because I had known I would win it before the tournament started."'

What an amazingly powerful picture he presents of the importance of picturing your goals. So it was on February 28, 2004 that I went to a bookstore at the top of Queen Street in Auckland. I'd been told that it was the biggest bookstore in the city, so went to see where my book would be. I found the business section and, as the books were laid out in alphabetical order, I found the spot where 'Hesketh' would be. I moved three of the books to one side to make a space for where my book would be on sale and stood back and pictured it.

I can see it now.

And as I stood six feet back from the fixture staring at this space in the bookstore, picturing my goal, I spotted another book I hadn't seen for some years. Norman Vincent Peale's *The Power of Positive Thinking* was written in 1953 and has sold over 15 million copies. I picked it up and although I had read it many years before, I thought it was time to buy a copy and re-read it. I looked at the price and it was NZ$31.95. I was in a relaxed frame of mind and looked at the opening pages. It explained that the book was initially written in 1953 and had been reprinted many times. I decided to read the preface, which, as you know, contains the very first words written in any book. This is what the opening paragraph in the book *The Power of Positive Thinking* says:

> At the time I wrote this book it never occurred to me that a
> two millionth copy anniversary would ever be observed.

I looked at the page and imagined Norman sitting at his old typewriter in 1953 working on the book. I could imagine his buddy calling to see him and asking what he was doing. I imagined Norman saying, 'I'm writing a book'. His buddy would naturally ask him what it was about and Norman would say, 'It's about the power of positive thinking. It's about beliefs. It's about how you can achieve more if you really and truly believe that you can do something'.

And I imagine his buddy saying that it was a fine thing to do. 'What are you going to call it, Norman?'

'*The Power of Positive Thinking.*'

'Excellent,' says his buddy. 'Do you think it will sell many copies?' And Norman would reply, 'No, not really'.

He didn't think a book called *The Power of Positive Thinking* would sell!

I also mentioned in Chapter 1 that this journey really began on the flight back from Harvard Business School with my colleague Bernie May sitting to my right and Paul Simpson, the then HR director of Arla Foods on my left. Paul asked me on that long flight home what it was I really wanted to do. I told him that I wanted to be a lecturer at Harvard. I told him that I wanted to speak at the likes of Cambridge and Oxford Universities. I told him that I would leave the agency on my 50th birthday to fulfil that dream. My colleagues were really helpful and 17 months later I went public on my goals. I spent two whole days telephoning clients, potential clients and key suppliers to the agency so that they would hear of my impending departure from the horse's mouth rather than from a third party.

One of my earliest telephone calls was to a client, Stephen Oliver, who was managing director of The Union Pub Company, part of Wolverhampton and Dudley Breweries. I'd always got on really well with Stephen and we'd shared some good times. I explained what it was that I was doing and he said, 'Are you available for bookings?'

Was I available for bookings? I had none!

He said he was having a management conference in 2003 and that he had faith in me to hold the attention of an audience for 45 minutes or so. Would I be interested in speaking at the conference? Of course I was delighted to be asked and said that I was flattered that he had faith in me. He explained the nature of the management conference and its objectives; he told me that I had a fairly free hand on what I said and how I said it, and it was only then that I asked him when and where the conference was as I didn't have one single booking for the whole of the year 2003.

'When is it?'

'It's on 10 April 2003.'

'Where is it?'

'It's at Oriel College, Oxford University. I'm an old boy of the college and have hired the college for our conference.'

I was born at 7.30 a.m. on April 10, 1953. My very first speaking engagement was to be on my 50th birthday at Oxford University.

I am certainly not making this up.

Isn't it amazing how if you have a clear goal, events conspire to help you towards it? Serendipity is a wonderful thing and I regarded that booking not just as the start of a new career but also a sign and confirmation that it was meant to be.

So what is motivation?

I was speaking at a conference at the International Convention Centre in Birmingham. I was to speak to over 300 delegates at 2 p.m.

for 35 minutes. I had my guitar on stage, the audience were beginning to come back in from lunch and I was getting ready for show time. The only thing that remained was for me to get my clip-on microphone from a young man called John who was behind the screen.

As I approached John, it was exactly six minutes to two and I asked if I could be miked up. He said to me, 'Are you the motivational speaker then?'

Now 'motivational speaker' is not an expression I use. I don't believe that motivation is something you can *do* to someone. I'm also concerned that if I'm on holiday and I'm asked what I do and I say I'm a motivational speaker they'll say, 'Well, go on then!'

But, with the audience filing in and me getting ready to speak and in the right mental state I took the easy option and said, 'Yes, I am'.

He said, in an insouciant drawl, 'Can you motivate me?' (and he did this in a Birmingham accent …)

So I said, glancing at my watch, 'What is it you want to do?'

And he said, 'I don't know; I just need motivating.'

I am not making this up.

But in many respects he summed it all up. Motivation is about having a goal. Motivation is about knowing what it is that you want to do (but not necessarily why you want to do it).

I believe that if you have the goal, and the emotional desire to achieve the goal, then you have motivation. And guess what? You can often get the ability later on.

I'm a fully paid-up member of Jane Tomlinson's fan club. She is, by her own description, 'an ordinary mother of three'. When she was diagnosed with a terminal illness in 2002 she was not given long to live. But she decided that she could achieve certain things before she died. She set herself the goal of running a marathon, then a triathlon 'Rome to Home'.

She raised hundreds of thousands of pounds in doing so because she had a goal. She had a goal, the emotional desire to achieve the goal and *then* she had motivation. The ability to run, cycle and swim came later. She cycled the 1905 miles from Rome to Leeds because she had a goal.

Karl Power had a picture and a goal or two. Karl is an ordinary lad from Droylsden near Ashton-under-Lyne. In April 2001 he and his mate Tommy went to Germany to watch Manchester United play Bayern Munich. At their hotel, they dressed up in full Manchester United kit before sneaking into the Olympic Stadium. As the two teams took to the field, Karl removed his tracksuit, ran on to the pitch behind his Manchester United heroes and lined up alongside them to have his photograph taken before kick-off.

The next day he was in just about every UK newspaper. In July 2001 he walked out in full England cricketer's kit to bat in the Ashes series. The plan went slightly awry because Tommy's signal was to be three rings on the mobile phone and unfortunately Karl's young niece called to see how the plan was going. He took it as the signal to walk on to the 'hallowed turf' despite the fact that two England batsmen were still in!

Made the news again, though.

In April 2002 he ran out with the England rugby team in Rome and in June 2002 he played tennis on the Centre Court at Wimbledon just before Tim Henman came on. And he was vilified by the press for wearing black socks! Finally, later that month, Karl, his mate Tommy and Tommy's son were photographed on the winners' podium at Silverstone in full Formula One driver's kit. I think they were only rumbled when they tried to cash the cheque.

Why? Even Karl doesn't know. The thing is, he had a picture. He had a goal, the emotional desire to achieve the goal and therefore he had the motivation. After that he found a way of achieving it.

Jane Tomlinson was told it wasn't possible for her to do a triathlon, run a marathon and cycle from Rome to Leeds. Karl was told by his friends it was a stupid thing to do and it wasn't possible. But where there's a will, there's a way.

When I set myself the goal of going to Harvard Business School, part of my motivation was to picture myself in the library at Harvard. On my first free Wednesday afternoon I went to the library just to sit there and read awhile to capture that magic moment. I went into the Widener library and I'd like to tell you the story of that too. Harry Elkins Widener came to England from the USA in 1912. He was something of a bibliographer and had come to England to buy books. Unfortunately his mode of transport back to the States was the doomed

Titanic. When the ship went down on 18 April he and his father, along with many of his books purchased, were lost. The story goes that he was about to step into a lifeboat that would have saved his life when he remembered a newly acquired book (apparently a copy of the second edition of Bacon's *Essais* from 1598) and ran back to get it. He was never seen again.

As a memorial to her son, the wealthy Mrs. Widener gave $2 million for the construction of a building that would house her son's collection so that he would be remembered forever. $2 million was a very large amount of money in 1912. If you ever get to Harvard I urge you to go to the library and to the small museum set aside to the memory of Harry Elkins Widener.

When I'm meeting with clients, often the managing director or sales director will talk to me about money being the ultimate motivator. Sometimes they say it's the *only* motivator but I don't believe that to be the case. Money is a hygiene factor. If people are being paid what they believe is their worth then it's often the feeling that they are being valued and recognized for their efforts that's more important than money. Of course, money *is* a motivator and it's certainly handy stuff when you go to the market, but there's far more to it than money.

So what are the six steps to success if we accept that motivation begins with having a goal?

1   Be passionate about what it is that you want to do. Have such an overwhelming, burning passion that it hurts.
2   Know the outcome and be able to measure it. Picture your goal so that you will know when you have achieved it. And don't be limited by what you know when you set your goal. Set your goals with 'no how' rather than 'know how'.
3   Be positive and talk about it. Or, as Linford Christie used to say, 'Go on the "b" of the bang'. Talk to other people who've done what you want to do and do what they do. Establish who can help you and talk to them about what it is you want to do and ask them for their help. You will then create an emotional 'pull' and, in turn, feel an obligation to carry out what you have said

you would do. Point being, if you don't want to make it public, you probably don't want it enough.

4   Take massive action and surprise your horse. I achieved my goal of speaking in New Zealand because I bought a ticket to go out there. Importantly, I bought the ticket before I had any work or anything remotely approaching a commitment from anybody to find me work. If you want to win the lottery, you have to buy a ticket. Take massive action that is different to what everyone else is doing. If everyone is zig-zagging you may have to zag-zig. Take massive action that says to your own subconscious, 'I have burnt my bridges. There is no way back.' When I embarked on my new career as a speaker I told everyone that I would not work in the advertising field again. I wanted to burn my metaphorical bridges.

5   Doggedness, tenacity and persistence are omnipotent. Or: 'If at first you don't succeed, neither did Kelly Holmes.'

6   Change your habits, your expressions and your expectations. Remember Professor David McClelland, who concluded that the single most important factor in people not achieving their goals was that they had the wrong friends? Avoid negative people and, if necessary, change the people around you. You become like the person you spend the most time with. And change your language. As we mentioned in Chapter 11, success in persuading and influencing is, itself, influenced by your own expectations. Expectation is also critical in negotiation; if you don't expect a top price and go for it, how can you possibly achieve it? And so it is with training your own subconscious. Not only do you need to retrain your horse to have higher expectation but you also need to stop saying certain things so that your horse (and by definition, you the rider) become more positive in outlook and expect to achieve more.

A friend of mine, Mike Marshall, was getting married on the banks of Loch Lomond and he and Trina kindly invited us to the wedding. Mike and I were having breakfast in Betty's, as we are wont to do, and I asked him how long it would take to drive from Harrogate to Loch

Lomond. 'An easy four hours, Phil.' Not 'four hours' – an 'easy' four hours. A simple expression that helps you feel good about the journey. For Mike, any walk seems to be a 'pleasant ten-minute stroll' even if it you need stout boots, a flask of hot tea and Kendal Mint Cake. So improve your language by talking about how much a client would be 'happy to invest' rather than simply ask his budget. Ask people to get *involved* rather than *commit*. Talk about *fees* rather than *commission*, talk *'form of payment'* rather than *card* or *cash*. Talk about *'particular issues to address'* rather than *'problems'*. Say 'I shouldn't tell you this but I will,' to engage and give the feeling of rarity.

Finally, in this chapter, here are the top ten things to stop saying if you really want to be more positive, more motivated and more motivating – and thereby more persuasive.

1 'I wish ...' Whenever you wish for anything you are saying to your own subconscious that you're not in control and only some higher being or 'Lady Luck' can help you. 'I wish I was slimmer' or 'I wish I had more money'. If you wish to win the lottery, buy a ticket.

2 'If only ...' How many times have you heard people say 'If only the client hadn't done that we could have achieved more' or 'If only I'd done things differently. I should have ...'? You did what you did and it's time to move on. Don't say 'If only ...', because you are saying to your own subconscious that you either should have done something in the past – which has gone forever – or that success is in someway conditional on something that's out of your control. And if you think it's out of your control, it is.

3 'I'll try ...' There is no try. There's do and don't do; there's can and can't; there's will and won't. If you asked me if I'd like to come to a party that you're organizing and I said 'I'll try and get there', I'm not coming, am I? Stop using 'try'.

4 'I don't have time.' Do you know that the average adult in Britain watches 24 hours of television every week? And most of the time most of those people are not watching something they planned to watch. Television is at the same time a great stimulator, entertainer and provider of information as well as being the greatest single

sapper of our time and energy. If you really want to achieve more, watch less television. Because that, as Joan Baez used to say, is where the time goes.

5   'I'm not too bad, really.' When asked how they are, people often go ahead and tell you, don't they?! If people ask how you are don't say, 'I'm not too bad, really' because what you're saying to your horse is that you *are* bad – you're just not too bad, really. So, as a consequence, your horse feels negative. Tell people that you're 'buzzing' or have never felt better or that you 'feel great today'. Not only does it cause a positive reaction in them, but all the time you're doing it, you're retraining your horse.

6   'You're wrong on that one.' Nobody likes to be told they're wrong, do they? Often people don't even need to be told at all – they know too.

7   'I told you so.' Again, people often know that *you told them so* and when the realization has just dawned is exactly the right time to start talking in positive terms rather than negative. If you do, they'll like you more and, as a consequence, they'll feel indebted to you. And we all know what that means.

8   'That's not my problem.' The mood and circumstance this can create in the listener is quite dramatic. Don't let your people feel they are not responsible

9   'Failure.' There is no failure – you just didn't get the result you were looking for this time. But you got a result and can learn from it.

10 'But …' There are, of course, some occasions to use it, *but* (!) reduce its usage by 80% and you will be more positive and persuasive. So often people use expressions such as, 'I'm not unsympathetic' or, 'I'm not one to gossip' and you *know* it will be followed by 'but' which completely negates the first part of the expression. Another real belter is 'With all due respect …' and it is known to both of you there is no respect at all.

CHAPTER 27

Feedback and its Importance

I am sitting in Pennyhill Park Hotel – a hotel I've made reference to before. As I am preparing myself to deliver a three-hour session, the hotel's managing director Danny Pecorelli approaches me. He introduces himself and we chat amiably. He asks if my stay is 'all right'. I say, 'No, Danny. It's not been all right.' I pause for just a second to create a 'special deal' – a hot and cold contrast – and say to him, 'It's way better than all right. It's probably the best hotel I've been in all year and the service is second to none.'

Danny thanked me for that and then he said a very interesting thing. 'Could you give me one area that we could improve on, Phil? Any aspect of the hotel or service where we could do better?' I thought long and hard and, quite frankly, couldn't come up with anything at all. 'Could you do me a really big favour, Phil, and give me one thing before you leave?'

My previous two nights had also been spent in hotels. They'll remain nameless to protect the innocent. But their service was nameless and, indeed, even aimless. Interestingly, no one asked me about the quality of the stay. Sometimes a hotel will send me a questionnaire asking for comments and I duly give them but I never, ever, get a response. They never tell me that it's been worthwhile and they never thank me for my time.

Interesting coincidence, don't you think?

The very best service from the best hotels also goes hand-in-hand with a desire to improve – a desire for feedback. People who don't offer a good service don't want to know about the feedback. Is it that they don't want to know how bad it is? Because, for sure, if you ask a question that you don't want the answer to you'd better expect an answer you don't like. But does it all come down to care? As we discussed in the last chapter, things are on the rise or on the wane. Nothing stays still forever – or as the French put it, 'Plus les choses changent, plus elles restent les mêmes.'

When you have made a presentation, how often do you ask for feedback whether or not you have won or lost the pitch you were making? How often do you ask your best friend to tell you the most irritating thing about you? If you truly want to be more persuasive and influential you've got to get the feedback on how you are. The most professional organization I consistently work with is TEC International. Not only are they extremely efficient and businesslike and, indeed, quite picky about which speakers they use, they also provide feedback after every single meeting. Members are encouraged to give the speaker something to work on.

Good speakers who want to be better love it. Average speakers who should be doing something else hate it. TEC tend not to use them.

Funny thing, isn't it?

It's what the Japanese call 'kaizen'. But in my experience of asking for feedback, people are often reluctant to give you their real feelings, particularly if you haven't been successful. If you're looking for a tip, ask them for three specific areas that you can 'work on'. For example, three things that if you were given the chance, you would have done differently.

When we pitched for the Dollond & Aitchison advertising account in the early 1990s it was at a time when opticians had just been given licence to advertise by the Government. Clive Stone, the chairman, Stephan Zagata and their team handled the whole thing very professionally and drew up a shortlist of four advertising agencies to pitch for the account. All the agencies were to present on one day in a hotel in Solihull near Birmingham. We were given the 'second slot' and a maximum of one and a half hours to present.

Dollond & Aitchison's logo was an owl and we had decided to make use of it. We made references to Lloyds Bank's black horse, Andrex's Labrador puppy, the Dulux Old English Sheepdog and so on. Yours truly thought it would be a good idea to have a real, live owl in the presentation and, although it didn't meet with widespread approval we decided, that, on balance, it could be a great idea.

Well, picture the scene. There are four of us suited and booted making our presentation to the five good people of Dollond & Aitchison. We have done one hour and twenty minutes of PowerPoint; we have run them through our research, explained our strategy and taken them through the creative work and media plans.

And now the pièce de résistance.

I had found a guy based in the West Midlands who had an owl. He seemed quite calm at 11 o'clock when we left him outside the room preening his charge and went to make our presentation. But, by 12.20, the guy was getting more and more nervous. At the risk of stating the obvious this was the first time he'd been involved in an advertising agency presentation for a multi-million pound account. So when I said with dramatic words 'and now the owl ...' and my colleague Bernie May opened the door, the man walked in with the owl. Not only was he petrified, worried and frightened, but he had transmitted his fear to the owl who promptly wanted to leave the room. I hadn't been in such close proximity to an owl before and I'm not in a hurry to do so again. It had a wingspan of about ten feet. And although it was tied to its keeper's gloved hand, it made a squawking noise that could be heard in nearby Solihull. Plus it flapped its wings with such drama and purpose that we all scattered to the corners of the room!

'Get it out, get it out!' cried Clive Stone, and, understandably, we ushered the man and his blessed owl away.

The five of us were silent on the drive home. We'd spent the thick end of three months preparing for this account and we were keen to win it. And this idea appeared to have blown the account and I was genuinely remorseful as I steered the car back up the M1. I was just glad we hadn't been pitching for the Lion Bar account because things could have turned out much worse.

When we got back to the office it had still not become funny. Do you find it interesting that so often something awful happens but it becomes really funny a month or two afterwards? Holidays that go wrong become funny stories later on.

Well, it wasn't funny yet.

By chance it was our board meeting that night and we started at 5.30 p.m. At 7.30 p.m. the phone rang – an odd event in itself. And it was Stephan Zagata. He wished to speak to me. My colleagues looked at me and I looked at them as I strode reluctantly to the telephone and picked it up. I felt certain he wanted to know how to get owl faeces off the upholstery and where to send the bill.

'You've won the account, Phil.'

Get in!

I made no reference whatsoever to the owl, but by midnight in the bar had convinced myself (and maybe even my colleagues) that it had been the inspiration that had clinched the account. It was the drama and purpose, it was the bit that made the difference. It was the feather-ruffling finale. I waxed lyrical and went to bed relieved and delighted.

The feedback?

Well, as always, win or lose I asked the client what we had done right and what we had done wrong. I also made a point of asking what other agencies had done to see if there was something we could learn.

It was ten days later that we dined in what was then La Locanda restaurant in Wetherby. Stephan and his team had come for the day and we'd all gone out for dinner. A joyous affair and an opportunity for the two teams to get to know each other. I sat next to Stephan over dinner and as we approached the brandies and coffees I asked him what the presentations had been like and if there was anything that we could learn.

'Well,' he began, 'you'd never believe it, Phil. One agency brought a bloody owl into the hotel room! We all had to scatter to the far corners. It was a ridiculous idea!' We laughed together and to this day Stephan doesn't know that he confused us with another agency. We'd got away with it. And how many times do you do that?

If you want to be truly persuasive and influential and you want to get better, you have to ask the questions to which you don't necessarily want the answers. You have to get feedback and take it on the chin.

These opportunities are all around us but we're not making the best use of them. We're not taking the time to learn, to develop and get better. We're not taking time to do the right things.

CHAPTER 28

Time Management

No book on what might loosely be described as 'self-improvement' would be complete without a chapter on time management, but I've distilled the whole thing down to five points:

1   Do what you say you are going to do.

Always. And do what you say you are going to do when you said you were going to do it and in the way that you said you were going to do it. In Chapter 11 we talked about expectations and how to manage them. In Chapter 19 we looked at how we all want a 'special deal', and how that 'reason' was at the centre of the seven and the fulcrum of how it all works. If you don't do what you say you are going to do, you are generating the very opposite of 'special deal'. You are losing credibility and eroding what trust the other person (or people) had in you. Conversely, if you over-deliver on a promise and go the extra mile you are building trust and credibility. And we all want, that don't we?

Living your life always doing what you say you are going to do has two enormous benefits. Firstly, your reputation is built on solid foundations and people will believe in you, trust you and like you. Secondly it makes you think more about the promises that you make. And that, in turn, makes for a happier life if you are not putting yourself under pressure you don't need to be under.

I am sitting on a bus that links Liverpool Street Station with London City Airport. On my arrival at the airport yesterday I specifically asked for a return ticket and ensured it was valid for a return the following day. And he said he would give me a return ticket. But he didn't. Maybe he kept the money; maybe I only paid for one way. Last week a man said he would definitely turn up to give us a quote for a new fireplace. But he didn't show. Another man was due to call round to quote to line the chimney – he didn't turn up – and the firm who have built our bathroom cabinets assured us in the most positive possible terms that the missing glass shelf would be with us 'within a week'. That was five months ago.

Why is it thus? Why do so many companies and their people not do the most basic – and most important thing in business – to do what they say they are going to do? I am at the airport. Deep joy – the plane is on time. I shall use this service again.

2 Create time for the things that are important both in your business and personal life but don't seem urgent right now.
(If you don't do them – if you don't allow time for planning – they grow and become more important, more urgent and any attempt at time management is lost).

3 Don't gossip. Don't blurt and don't talk about people when they are not there unless it's glowing praise.

4 Differentiate between the time that makes you money (seeing clients, telephoning prospects, agreeing deals etc.) and the time that doesn't (internal meetings, admin etc).
See a line between the two with all the admin 'stuff' on the left and the making money time on the right. Always know what side of the line you are on and keep on the right side as much as you can.

5 Know when your prime time is and do your prime jobs then.
We all have different circadian rhythms. Do your most important jobs when you are at your best. And don't just choose to do the easy, 'nice' jobs first.

CHAPTER 29

Making Sense of It All

I once ran a competition for potential clients where the reward for responding was to be entered into a free prize draw to see the diminutive Irishman, Chris de Burgh in concert in Birmingham. There were nine pairs of tickets to be won and, with my wife and I, the twenty of us would have a special hospitality area at the NEC, watch the concert and then come back to have dinner. It was a worthwhile prize and I notified all the winners by telephone at around 10 o'clock one morning.

Needless to say, they were all delighted and I was just leaving the agency that lunchtime when the receptionist said there was a call for me. It was from one of the winners of the prize. 'I don't know how to tell you this Phil, but since you called me I've been hauled into the managing director's office and I've just been made redundant. I am devastated. I should let you know this because obviously I don't really qualify for the two tickets any more.'

I didn't even need to think about it. He'd won the prize and the last thing I was going to do to a man who'd just had such bad news was exacerbate the problem by telling him he wasn't welcome at a Chris de Burgh concert.

I reassured him that not only would he and his wife be still very welcome but that if there was anything I could do to help him in his career I would be delighted to do so. However, since he was no longer strictly speaking a potential client, I would have to charge him £75 plus postage for the tickets. Only kidding.

He and his wife came along to the concert and we chatted. By this stage he'd got a new job and things were looking good and I was delighted for him.

Now fast-forward six months.

I received a phone call out of the blue. Would I like to meet the marketing director of what was then Halifax Insurance, Neil Utley? It wasn't a potential client I was particularly targeting but I was more than happy to meet Mr Utley. The conversation was with his secretary and we fixed an appointment and I turned up at his offices in Halifax. His secretary came to meet me and ushered me up the stairs. She said, 'You don't remember me, do you?' And I apologized and said that I didn't.

'You were very good to my husband some months ago. He'd been made redundant and it made a big difference to him that you still wanted us to go to the Chris de Burgh concert.' By then, of course, I'd remembered her and that we had had an enjoyable conversation. She then said to me, 'I said to him at the time if ever I can do something for that guy Phil Hesketh, I'll do it. And when my boss Neil Utley said he wanted to speak to some advertising agencies about direct mail you were my first thought.'

Neil and I have gone on to become good friends and he became a client of the agency and, indeed, has become a client of mine as chief executive of Cox Insurance.

And it all came down to one opportunity to be honest and sincere and genuine and making a straightforward decision.

You reap what you sow.

Red dress or black dress?

Naturally, for Chris de Burgh it would be the red dress that has made him millions, but for most of us men deciding what to wear on an evening is a reasonably straightforward procedure. Firstly, there's whether it's casual, formal or black tie; and secondly, we need to make sure that we wear the right colour shoes. And for some men that's about it.

If like me, you're a man and you're married to a woman, you may have wondered what to do when she says, 'Should I wear the red dress or the black dress?'

There are five key steps in the process and finishing up with a happy outcome. Follow these steps with assiduity.

1   Be very, very interested in whether it's the black dress or the red dress. If you are not actually interested, do your best to fake it. Glance away from the newspaper momentarily at the very least.
2   Be as indecisive as her, as this creates empathy.
3   Importantly, ask her which dress *she* prefers.
4   This is the most important step: ask her *why* she prefers one dress over the other.
5   Agree with her.

This needs to take a little time. If you rush it you appear to be insincere and uninterested and you need to go back to step one again.

WHAT DOES INFLUENCE MEAN?

Influencing and negotiating. What do they actually mean? They're interesting words and it's worth looking at what they mean in their original etymology. The word influence means 'to flow into'. So think of the influence as a river and the influencer as a stream. And think of how natural it is in nature.

If a stream meets up with a river it joins the current of the river and flows in the same direction. It rarely begins to influence the course of the river until it has established the current. Of course, if the stream is big and strong and the river is small and weak it can bulldoze, as we said in Chapter 12. But you are reading this book because you need to be a 'burgeoner'. And *that* word means to grow and flourish. Influence is about seeing things from the other person's point of view. It's about joining in and listening carefully to objections. It's about asking questions and accepting the answers before you exert your influence.

Interestingly, if man tries to alter the course of a river he builds a dam across it. And what happens? In pushing it into another path the river reverts to its original course as soon as it possibly can. And if for some reason it can't do that, then untold damage is caused behind the dam as the river builds up. You reap what you sow.

Unless you are 'pushing an open door', influencing doesn't work that way. That's why you need to establish the other person's need(s) and work from that as the starting point. Just as the river joins the stream and has to slowly but surely work out the pace, direction and force of the stream before it can truly begin to influence.

As we continue to look at things that matter to the other person, we need to consider what their priorities are. What are the things that are important to them? In order to do this we need to step into their shoes. This is a strange expression and yet perhaps one we should take more literally. What would it *feel* like to be in their position? What are the things that matter to them? Rather than trying to second-guess it, put yourself into their position.

There's a song by Bob Dylan, 'Positively 4th Street'. In it he sings:

> Yes, I wish that for just one time,
> You could stand inside my shoes.
> Then you'd know what a drag it is to see you.

Imagine hating somebody that much! You hate someone so much you want them to be in your shoes so that they could truly feel how you feel when you see them! It's the exact opposite of empathy, isn't it?

As your persuadee is speaking to you, use *their* language when you respond. If someone says to you, 'Well, I'm fed up because you can't get anything done round here', don't turn to them and say, 'what makes you so annoyed about it?' They haven't said that they were annoyed, they said that they were 'fed up because they can't get anything done round here'; so use their words back to them. Use the same sort of language rather than imposing your own way of saying what they say. If you want to have an influence the first thing to do is enter the river of the other person and learn how the current is flowing and go in the same direction. Using the same language is a key indicator to them that you understand them.

Or, in other words, go with the flow.

Time passes at the same rate; 60 seconds a minute. Doesn't always feel like that, does it? The time that has passed never comes back. So respect your time here. After all, you're just passing through. And remember to have a certain respect for other people's time.

I don't want to work in a biscuit factory again – but I'm glad I did. I want to go to Kansas City to see if everything is up to date there. I want to go to Alexandria and have an ice-cold beer. I want to go to Nashville and play the guitar. I want to drive down Route 66 and see if I can get my kicks there. I want to know why there is no blue food. I want to meet a Wichita Lineman. I want to sail on *Kon-Tiki*. I want to fly with the eagles. I want to swim with dolphins. I want to go for it all or die trying. I want to play live with Ralph McTell. I want to change the weather in February. I want to be a professor at Harvard. I want this to be a best-selling book. And I want to be the best speaker on the planet. Happiness is the journey, not the destination. You have to believe you can and at the same time marry that with the discipline to confront the fact that you are sometimes physically or mentally not able to fulfil a dream; so do what you can and move on.

Here are my ten final thoughts:

I Gain respect

By and large people are not influenced by people they don't respect. So work hard to gain that respect before you attempt to exert persuasion. Football managers hopeful of signing a new player do it all the time. They talk in the press about his 'great qualities' and how he would be 'an asset to any team'. Then they start the persuasion. And when the player *does* become a member of the squad he *wants* to play for the manager – he is *motivated*. So be sure to find out what a person is really good at and tell them so – particularly if it's a loved one.

2 Establish emotional, psychological needs

Everybody has their own particular needs. Yours is to persuade someone to do something. However, you must be patient at the outset and establish the other person's needs first of all. Do this by asking questions and accepting the answers. Headlines in ads for medical products almost always ask a question because it immediately gets the reader into a positive and receptive frame of mind. 'Do you suffer from memory loss?'; 'Having difficulty sleeping at night?'; 'Tense, nervous, headache?'; and my own personal favourite, the world's greatest one-word headline, 'Piles?' You get the idea.

3 Empathize

Establishing the other person's needs is just the beginning of the persuasive process. You then have to take this information on board and understand the implications for them of what it is you want them to do, think or buy into. For instance, if a one-legged man came into your shoe shop and tried on a sandal, you wouldn't offer to get the other one for him, would you? So ask people to explain their worries and truly empathize with them before you comment. And stop worrying about what people think about you. Because *they* don't know what *you* know.

4 Move into the inner circle but don't get too near the violins

Allow me to explain.

In an orchestra the musicians sit in a semi-circle. The conductor is in the centre – what I will refer to as the 'close circle'. Right at the edge of the circle are the drums. Big guys with that strange leopard skin tied around the mid-riff and on that, a drum. All manner of people making a noise, but on their own not very tuneful as anyone who has had a child with a drum kit will testify.

Then as you move towards the conductor the next instruments are the trumpets, trombones, French horns and tubas. A bit more interesting to listen to but, again, on their own not easy on the ear.

Then it gets more interesting. As you get nearer to the conductor you get bassoons and then the flutes, oboes, piano and harps. And finally you get the violas, cellos and the violins. Ah, yes, the violins.

And so it is with your relationships. If you want to be persuasive imagine the person you want to persuade being the conductor. After all, that is the person with the money. And all the money you will ever have in the future is currently in the hands of someone else. You need to move into their 'circle' – the 'inner circle'. If you don't form any emotional bond and don't truly empathize you are just a loud drum. You make a noise but no one wants to listen. As you move closer by establishing the emotional bond then you start making music you both enjoy.

But be careful not to get too close. Beware of getting in there with the violins where they can pull on your heartstrings. Beware of getting in the 'close circle'. Work colleagues who socialize and get to know each other's families often have a problem discussing an issue. Sales people who get too close to their buyers often find it difficult to move back into harsh commercial reality and deliver bad news. They tend to be too soft on negotiation to the extent that they forget whom they work for.

So establish the other person's emotional needs and have genuine interest and empathy. But you can get too near to the flame. We all need people who we can play the violin with and they with us. But be aware that's a different type of relationship.

5 Learn to say 'no' politely

If you want to truly influence an outcome then you have to be in control of the situation as early as possible. That usually means subtly dictating the topic of conversation. Setting the parameters. Establishing the rules. Defining the ballpark. You need to appear firm without giving the impression of being ruthless. Which means learning to say 'no' politely. Prefixing your answer with a compliment is just one way of softening the blow. For example, 'I can see your point and fully understand your request. I get frustrated too that the market sets the price and the painstaking production process dictates the delivery date' is a much better answer than, 'No you can't have it cheaper or sooner'. Learn to say 'no' to yourself too. We all need to recognize when we have done 'enough'.

6 Use the carrot more than the stick

We have talked a lot about motivation and seeing things from the other person's point of view. We have looked at our cavemen, the farmer and the 'burgeoner'. We have looked at the triangle of relationships, so let's look at one last triangle – the triangle of influence and persuasion and the role of the carrot and the stick (see Figure 29.1). The difference between being a 'boss' and being a 'leader' is, in the author's view, a simple one. You work for a boss and you do what you have to do because you *have* to do it. You do what you do for a leader because you *want* to do it. And that's why leaders are held in high esteem and bosses with contempt. The most basic way of persuading and influencing is to use the stick. It assumes a level of fear. Better than that is

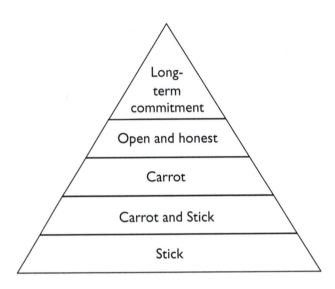

Figure 29.1 *Triangle of influence and persuasion*

the combination of carrot and stick. Better than that is just carrot, and the ability to appear to only be using the carrot to motivate is that you have developed an open and honest relationship with your colleague or buyer. And when you do that you get a long-term commitment.

7 Know your goals
It's impossible to measure your own effectiveness if you don't know what your objectives are. So be sure to have some and always keep them in mind. They could be material or spiritual, or a mix of both. Personally, I would never work for the money alone. The only person who gets job satisfaction from that is your bank manager.

Imagine you are going to die soon and have been granted one last phone call. Who would you call and what would you say to them? And if it's that important, why are you waiting?

8 Enjoy the journey
Remember that happiness isn't the destination, it's the journey. So be sure to have a valid ticket and don't forget to look out of the window occasionally. Work to live, don't live to work. Or as my wife likes to say, 'Put that away now and come to bed.'

If you haven't yet found love in your life, don't give up. Look at Peter Stringfellow. That should cheer you up. And remember, no matter how hard you try, you can't look for love without getting hurt. It just wouldn't be fair on the rest of us.

9 Be yourself

Don't just do what everyone else is doing. They're all looking to take their lead from someone else anyway. Stay focused on your own life and goals, and don't get worked up over small, insignificant things. If it really troubles you, see a doctor.

Remember, if you want to influence people, you need to win friends. If you want to win friends, you must learn to see things from the other person's perspective. If you want to see things from the other person's perspective, you need to ask questions. And when you ask questions, be prepared to accept the answers.

10 Write a desiderata

Last but not least, write your own 'desiderata'. Not only for yourself but also for your children's children's children. Mine is set out as the appendix to this book. In Latin it means 'that which is lacking or wanted'. In English, we call it a wish list. It doesn't guarantee happiness or success, but it will help you to define it for yourself. That's the first step to making something happen.

CHAPTER 30

The End of the Beginning or 'Nice is Expensive'

It is early on Wednesday February 23, 2005 and I am sitting overlooking Takapuna bay, just over the Harbour Bridge from Auckland, New Zealand. The sun is coming up over Rangitoto Island and a ferryboat glides slowly along in the distance. An early morning walker ambles by with her dog and the world is at one. It looks like it will be a lovely summer's day with just a little cloud.

I am *absolutely* not making this up.

I am about to embark on a two-day programme on the psychology of persuasion. At the end of the two days I will launch the first version of this book – entitled *Life's a Game So Fix the Odds*. It has been an interesting journey and I am on an interesting path.

It is nice to be here but it has, of course, cost money and effort to get to this point where I have changed the weather in February.

For me.

So what has this book been about? Why it is worth making the effort to be more persuasive or, to put it another way, 'nicer'?

Because 'nice' comes expensive.

Why do we pay such a premium for the interior lights in our car to 'dim' rather than simply switch off after a few seconds? Why do we pay a premium for cup holders in our cars that have that nice 'swooosh' sound as they open? Why are the ladies who sell cosmetics so polite and well groomed? Why do people pay such a premium for first class travel? Why do expensive shops go to such lengths to create a relaxing and delightful environment? How can certain cafés and bars charge a premium for a drink as simple as a cup of tea or a glass of beer? How are they able to 'persuade' you?

Because 'nice' is expensive and expensive is nice.

Why are budget airlines staff downright rude? Why do people who work in discount stores not care about service? Why do staff in inexpensive hotels and motels not ask whether (and how) they can improve their offer? Transient employees often move on because they can see something better. Sometimes they leave because they are not 'treated' well. Why do pretty much all service companies in countries with low unemployment struggle to get cheap labour to give good service?

Because 'nice' people are more expensive.

And that's why it pays to be nice. Because people are willing to pay for 'nice'. People are willing to pay a premium for design, for a belief in a brand, for 'service' – and for 'service' read 'nice'.

We buy emotionally and justify logically.

To paraphrase Winston Churchill, is this the beginning or the end for you? Or is it the end of the beginning? Will you live your life in a more persuasive and 'nicer' way from now on? For me it is simply the end of the beginning.

I have made some progress on playing live with Ralph McTell – I have talked about him at every seminar and conference I have spoken at. I will meet him one day and perhaps achieve my goal. But what *then*? What do I do from *that* point on? Plan to play with Sting? Or Eric Clapton?

Happiness is the journey, not the destination.

I have made some progress on becoming the best and most sought-after speaker on the planet – bar none; I look forward to speaking at Harvard, Oxford (again), Cambridge and Yale Universities. I have written the best-selling book and, of course, I have changed the weather in February.

The sun is up now. New Zealanders are beginning their day. It's time to begin mine.

Life's a game and this book helps you fix the odds. Provided you *do* the stuff. It's time to spin the wheel and place your bets. Good luck.

Philip's Desiderata

Go placidly amongst the noise and haste and all that. Be happy that there are some things you cannot change. Happiness only comes when you accept the things you cannot influence.

Separate opinion from fact but don't let facts
get in the way of a good story.

Also separate whites from coloureds, unless you live alone.

Today is the first day of the rest of your life. Do something as though it were the last day of your life.

'Hang around' sometimes – learn to watch ants and think about why they do all that running around.

Make friends with freedom and uncertainty.

Cry during movies. But only during the soppy bits.
And do it quietly.

Assume that anyone driving faster than you and agitating you is suffering some sort of disaster and needs to go that fast.

Stuff happens – true contentment comes from
reacting positively to it.

Never stop hugging your kids. That way they still
hug you when they're bigger than you. Which is nice.

Never outstay your welcome. Like the Spanish say:
guests and fish both begin to smell after three days.

Never book a short break to Spain of more than three days.

Discourage small children from walking around
with sharp objects.

Do the same with big children.

Swing as high as you can on a swing by moonlight.

Walk into the sea with your clothes on at midnight.
Only do it once and somewhere warm.

Do it for love.

Do it now. The money will follow.

Make people laugh. Wear a Paisley shirt with a striped tie.

Do something crazy with custard once in a while.

Read every day. But not out loud.

Learn new words – you can chew them.

Giggle with children.

Say 'Bula' when you arrive home. Every day.
Refuse all requests for an explanation.

Don't eat sprouts unless there's someone standing over you.

Don't buy things you don't need with money you haven't
got to impress people you don't like.

Always have clean shoes – it says a lot about you.

Write your own desiderata for your children's grandchildren.

Listen to those older than you are.
They're getting fewer in number every day.

Write little notes saying nice things to good friends
expecting nothing in return.

If you can't be with the one you love, honey;
love the one you're with.

Love the one you're with.

Remember: if you're not the lead husky you only ever get one view.

Don't take your shirt off on stage. It's not big and it's not funny.

Remember the total result of all of your ambition
is to be happy in your own head.

With all its sham, drudgery and broken dreams, it is still
a beautiful world. Be cheerful. Strive to be happy.

Spot every gorgeous moment and be sure to celebrate each one.

Index